D1246734

The Adventures of Snowshoe Thompson

About the Book

The snowshoes that he fashioned himself are known as skis today. But skis were unknown on the frontier, and when John Thompson made the odd-looking slats, they were called "gliding shoes" or "snow skates" and finally "snowshoes." That was 1856, and for years thereafter, the only mail that crossed the California Sierra Nevadas in wintertime was the mail in the eighty-pound sacks carried on the back of Snowshoe Thompson.

A.
ORBAAN

The Adventures of Snowshoe Thompson

by Curtis W. Casewit • Illustrated by Albert Orbaan

Editorial Consultant

Edna B. Ziebold, San Diego County Department of Education

G. P. Putnam's Sons • New York

Library of Congress Catalog Card Number: 73-102395
PRINTED IN THE UNITED STATES OF AMERICA
10212

Contents

The Colorful and Exciting

SAGAS OF THE WEST

From G. P. Putnam's Sons

First Wagons to California
by Michael Chester — Illustrated by Steele Savage

Colonel Anza's Impossible Journey
by Jonreed Lauritzen — Illustrated by Steele Savage

Flag of the Dreadful Bear
by Robert West Howard — Illustrated by Albert Orbaan

Forts of Old California
by Michael Chester — Illustrated by Steele Savage

The Battle of San Pasqual
by Jonreed Lauritzen — Illustrated by Leon Gregori

Joseph Strauss: Builder of the Golden Gate Bridge
by Michael Chester — Illustrated by Tom Hamil

The Adventures of Grizzly Adams
by Jean Muir — Illustrated by Albert Orbaan

The San Francisco Earthquake and Fire
by Helen Markley Miller — Illustrated by Albert Orbaan

The Adventures of Snowshoe Thompson
by Curtis Casewit — Illustrated by Albert Orbaan

Acknowledgments

During the three years of researching and writing this book, I ran up a debt to many people. I must thank Robert Parker, of Vail, Colorado, for suggesting a Thompson book in the first place. Thanks go to Irving Stone, whose *Men to Match My Mountains* confirmed the story and provided some of the background. I'm indebted to the Bancroft Library in Berkeley, California, and to the Western History Department, Denver Public Library. While writing this biography, I called on Gerry Groswold, son of a ski maker; Aylesa Forsee, author; Jackson Dyson, state park historian; Frances Clow, librarian; and Lars Langaker, cultural attaché, Norwegian Embassy. All have earned my gratitude.

The book would have been difficult to do without the generosity of Art Wood, Crystal Bay Development Company, Incline Village, Nevada.

John "Snowshoe" Thompson

The Adventures of Snowshoe Thompson

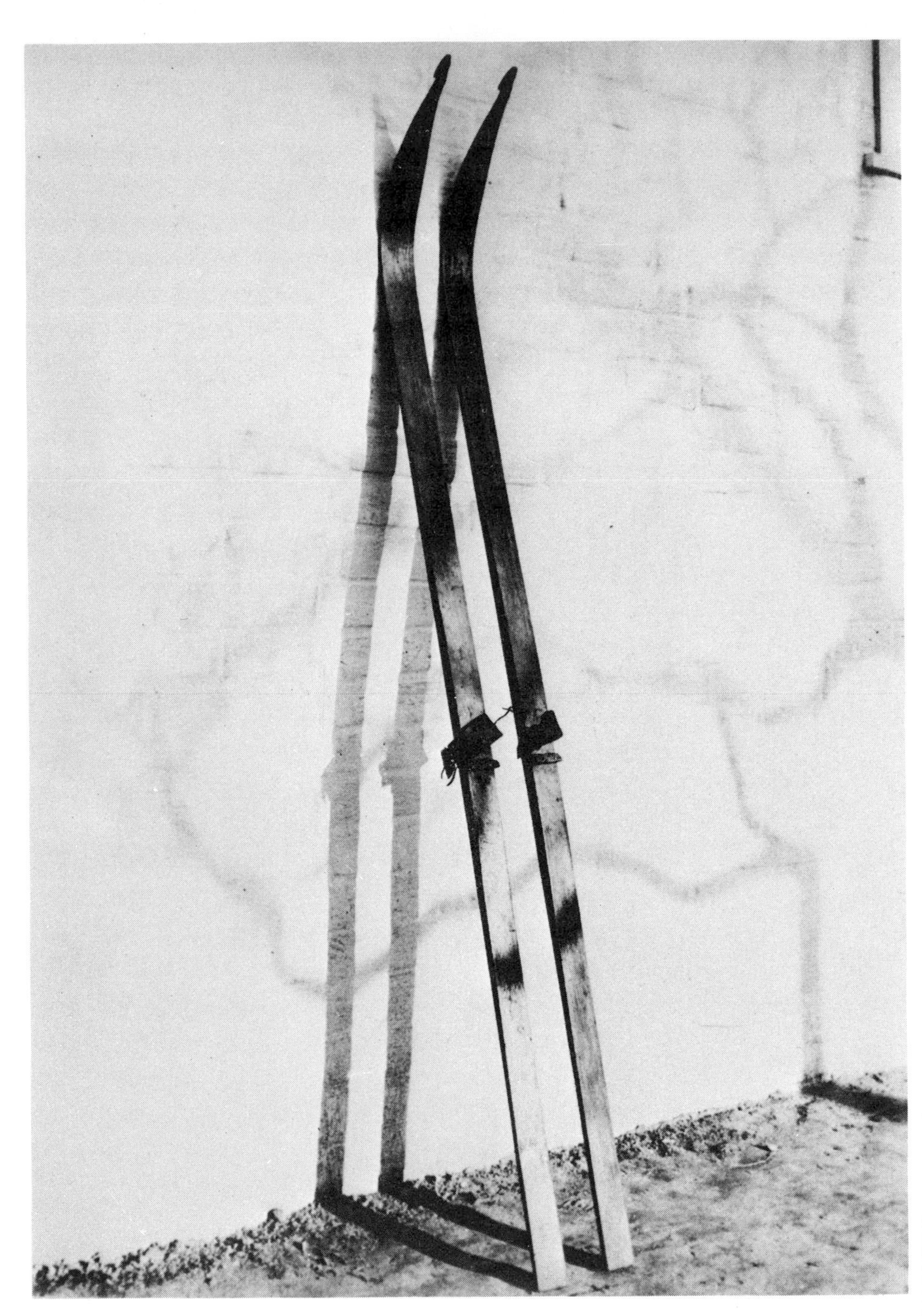

Thompson's skis

I The Job

NO ONE saw him that November morning. His small farm in the Sacramento Valley of California was far enough from other people. He worked alone, and for now, he worked in secret.

Silently he drew something on paper. Crossed it out. Began again. After sketching for an hour, he hurriedly left his log cabin. He had the tools of the Old West: a sharp ax to fell a tree, an adze to cut off the branches and smooth the wood, and an auger to bore holes. Soon the chinks flew from an oak that bordered his field. The air smelled sweet with sawdust. He hacked and whittled away until he had two long boards. When stood on end, they reached higher than his outstretched hands. He was a tall man, a six-footer, with long legs, long arms, and long fingers that could build and fix and shape. Born in Norway as Jon Torsteinson Rui, he called himself John Thompson. Later, he would be known as Snowshoe Thompson.

He worked faster now, his blue eyes agleam, his ruddy face flushing with pleasure. Yes, the memory of his Scandinavian boyhood was coming back to him. He carved the tips of the two wooden staves until they looked almost like lances, then drilled small holes into them. He boiled some water and stuck the tips in. After about an hour, the wood was soft enough to bend with ease when Thompson pulled at the string that ran through the tip holes. Good. The oak curved upward. He took the steaming staves out of the water and leaned them against his cabin to cool.

A few days of drying, and he was almost ready. He sanded the bottoms of the boards to smoothness. He fastened a pair of leather thongs that would fit over a man's boots.

He had built two Scandinavian snowshoes (today they are called skis). One afternoon in December, Thompson shoved his new skies into a canvas bag, saddled his horse, and slung the bag across his broad shoulders. To town!

Presently, he rode through the few acres he owned along Putah Creek toward Placerville, California.

There, at Snyder's General Store, Thompson weighed the bag and its contents. Twenty-five pounds. Heavy. The store was full of people; near the scales they prodded Thompson to show what he had. He slowly pulled out the ten-foot-long boards. From behind a flour barrel, Snyder asked, "What are they for?"

"For the mountains," another Norwegian explained.

"Gliding shoes!" someone said.

"Snow skates!"

Thompson wasn't one to talk much. In the first place, he'd fashioned his snowshoes for a private reason. And second, he still didn't know if he could make them work. He would try before the sun went down behind the wooded hills. So he mounted his horse once more and rode through the unpaved muddy streets. The town was alive with miners. They made a lot of noise in the saloons. They went into small hotels, carrying bedrolls. They led burros loaded with picks, shovels, buckets,

and pans. They pushed wheelbarrows with other gear for gold seeking. Thompson saw them slipping in and out of the assayer's office, and behind the windows of their shacks. He saw a family loading a covered wagon, bound for Sacramento—or perhaps San Francisco?—the next day. People moved a lot in those days, and Placerville faces changed as quickly as the names of a town. Not too long ago, the town had been called Dry Diggings, then Hangtown, because some criminals had been hung here, and now it was Placerville.

Bundle across his shoulders, Thompson waved to the people. He hadn't married yet, but he liked children. Then the roofs were below him, like so many helter-skelter toys. The mountain's snowline had begun. When the snow got deep, Thompson tied his horse to a tree and took the skis out of the bag, but he did not yet put them on. It was a struggle to climb with the heavy skis on his shoulders. And the higher he got, the harder it was to move. Soon he sank in to his knees. When he found a flat spot, it was time to stop and strap on his 25-pound snowshoes.

He carefully planted them in the snow, pushing until only the tips stuck out. Now he scraped the bottom of one boot and slid it into the binding, right under the rawhide strap, then did likewise with the other foot. He stood. He had learned to use snowshoes as a boy in Norway's Telemark County.

His father had brought him to America when he was ten, and the family, including a brother and sister, had settled in the Midwest. There had been no chance to use skis in Illinois and Missouri, and since coming West in 1851, Thompson had not tried to use them either. In fact, he hadn't attempted anything like this since boyhood.

Could he still do it?

He had to; there was more at stake than anyone knew. Thompson lifted one leg above the snow, then the other. The weight was terrible. He pushed one tip through the snow. Heading slightly up the hill, he let the next tip follow. To his surprise, he suddenly slipped backward. He came to a stop where he'd been in the first place. He tried again, stamping down hard, and in this manner gained a few yards. In Norway, Thompson's father had never slid and slipped back. But how was it done?

All at once, Thompson remembered that he should put the skis down like two spokes of a wheel, or like the bones of a long fish. Climbing now proved less slippery. It was still hard work, though, and Thompson began to sweat as he toiled through the trees. He inched still higher. He entered a glade and crossed it, skis side by side now. But he still looked awkward. It was a clumsy business, and Thompson must have realized that he had forgotten one important item. That was a long pole. With a pole, a man could pull himself up at every step, and a pole prevented backward sliding. Thompson's father had always used one in Scandinavia.

At last, Thompson reached the top of a knoll. Ready for the downhill trip! Ready for the easy part! He pointed his tips toward the valley. For a moment the skis were slow. But after a few yards they picked up the speed of a lance soaring from a mountaintop. Thompson plunged steeply down the glade and promptly fell. It did not hurt, but his hat had flown off. His blond hair and his blond beard were full of wet snow. Snow had crawled down his neck. Snow had crept into his high boots. He got up, shivering. He skied farther down. Again he stumbled and fell. It was almost dark when he reached his house.

The next day Thompson whittled a long pole from a sapling.

But on the way up, the 25 pounds of oak still felt more like 25 pounds of lead. The runners seldom obeyed during these first attempts. Thompson was glad that the townspeople minded their own affairs far below. They would surely laugh at the cocoon of snow on him each time he tumbled. If they saw him, he reckoned, they would smile at the fatigue in his blue eyes. And they might guess at the pain in his legs.

But he was powerfully built, with muscles that were used to strain. He had good lungs and a strong heart, farm-bred shoulders, and no body fat to carry around. As a youth he had helped his parents do the heavy fieldwork, and then had done a lot of it at Putah Creek. So after some days he got less and less tired, and he made speedy progress with his snowshoes. He soon learned to control them, uphill or down. He learned to bend his knees a little on the descents, learned that he was much safer with a wide track, legs well apart. He learned how to make good use of the pole, too. Diving downhill, he would hold it across his chest for balance. To reduce speed he would push it into the snow like a rower straightens an oar in the water to bring a boat to a stop.

It was all a matter of practice.

At first, Thompson was alone on the mountain. The silence was sweet to him; the air was full of pine scents; the light on the snow changed every hour. But after a week a few Placerville folks came to the mountain in search of firewood and game. They discovered Thompson's doings.

The news spread and people were mystified. They'd seen webbed, oval-shaped snowshoes, the kind used by the Indians and Canadians. The slow kind. But few people had seen skis.

"Hey!" the miners shouted.

Thompson flew down the hillsides at great speeds now. He floated on snow like a Viking ship on high seas. He climbed without a pause; he plunged down, ducking under trees, turning, and stopping at will. A Placerville settler even saw Thompson take jumps. Five feet, then ten feet, finally twenty feet. Each time, he landed with ease and sped on. As another week went by, there were more and more spectators. Placerville's youngsters were the most curious of all. How could a man manage such speeds? Would he hurt himself soon? Why did he risk so much?

The town was all talk now. What did Thompson intend to do with his mysterious skill? *What was he up to?*

They asked him in Placerville, they asked him in Sacramento, and they asked him everywhere in between. But he said little.

Thompson didn't set out to become a legend. Fame came later. Fame for saving lives, thanks to his skis. Because of his incredible daring, a postage stamp eventually bore his picture. In the Sierras a ski race was later named for him. And soon the newspaper reporters would be eager to describe his adventures.

Yet heroism was far from Thompson's mind when he shot down the Placerville slopes. He just wanted to perfect his skill to get through any kind of terrain in winter quickly.

His reasons were easy to understand. For a long time, people in all the United States territories and states were complaining about the slow mail service. Families in New York, Chicago, St. Louis, and elsewhere had petitioned the government to improve the speed of letters. They had cause for complaints: in the 1850's mail from Boston to San Francisco could take a full year. Because of Indian raids and other dangers on land, a letter often went all the way via Panama on muleback or horseback. Worse, some packages from East to West coasts traveled by ship in a full circle around South America. In winter the connection between the two U.S. coasts was even less reliable because of two mighty mountain chains. Coming from the East, a man had to cross the formidable Rocky Mountains, battling a height of 14,000 feet, then the forbidding Sierra Nevadas. And Thompson knew that at this time of the year mail between the high mining towns often wouldn't be delivered at all.

Roads were crude in those days, and no one would have known how to clear the snow masses. Stagecoaches could never make it. And no railroads had yet spanned that region.

The Placerville postmaster was therefore in desperate need of a mail carrier. Thomson had read about it in a Sacramento paper. He'd also read that the winter ahead would be an especially grim one, with bone-chilling blizzards that kept men by their firesides for weeks. Snows would lie 40 feet deep. Placerville would be shut off. All contact between the settlements would be lost unless someone came forward with enough courage and stamina to hurdle the icy spine of the Sierras carrying the mail. A man unafraid of a 100-mile trek in subzero weather. Somebody who didn't fear Indians on the warpath or hungry wolves or wild bears. A person who didn't mind solitude. Not only the post office but all of Placerville and the other snowbound communities waited for a man to dare the wilderness.

John Thompson was that man.

On his skis he woud become the link between human beings during four or more harsh winter months. Norway produced him, with those blue eyes and blond hair and the strength and stubbornness to go with it. But the American West gave him a chance to become the subject of a saga.

In January, 1856, Thompson was ready. He figured that he could hurdle any mountain stretch on his "snowshoes." And at the age of twenty-eight, thanks to his many workouts, he was at the peak of his physical condition.

He took his man-high boards to the post office. Bins of mail stood on the floor, where they might wait for months now. In winter couples often were wed here without being able to tell their parents in Chicago about it. Babies might be four months old by the time the birth announcement finally reached St. Louis. People made and lost fortunes on both sides of the Sierras without their closest friends learning about it. A boy who had gone West from Pennsylvania might be in terrible need of money, yet he couldn't tell his parents about it in time for help. Worse, sometimes miners had died of illness before a letter was finally delivered. Thompson had lived through the anguish of a delay himself. Just recently he had received a letter from his father. It had taken three months from Illinois to California. The letter had brought sad news: Thompson's mother had died of influenza. With the slow, slow mails, John Thompson's words of sorrow and comfort would reach his father much too late.

Thompson showed his equipment to the post office clerk, who thought him a little mad. Norsky snowshoes?

Impossible.

Eighty-pound sacks to be carried on a human back for five cold days?

Unbelievable.

Still, the clerk fetched Allen M. Thatcher, the postmaster.

Thompson had saved the newspaper story in the Sacramento *Union* which had brought him here. The headline read: PEOPLE LOST TO THE WORLD! UNCLE SAM NEEDS MAIL CARRIER!

Mr. Thatcher looked doubtful but friendly. He cocked his head. Wouldn't Thompson get lost, too, in the wintry terrain?

"I can go anywhere in the mountains," Thompson replied softly.

"Day and night?"

"Yes," Thompson said. "Day and night. Storm or shine."

"It's ninety miles to Genoa."

Thompson nodded.

"You'd find the way?"

"A man can. If he has his wits about him."

Mr. Thatcher still looked doubtful. But he was willing to listen.

The Norwegian spoke good English, but he spoke slowly. He was a man who had been alone much and had found little need to sell himself to others. Still, as he stood there, tall and lean, looking straight into Mr. Thatcher's eyes, Thompson made a good impression.

He could read and write, Thompson said.

He'd trapped animals and grown wheat. He'd ridden much,

and in the last few years he'd also been a mountain guide. He'd led people through the Sierras on foot whenever horses couldn't make it. In between, he'd hiked to all the mining camps. Genoa. Carson Valley. Virginia City. Strawberry Flat. He knew the route across the passes. He had his own landmarks. He knew rock shelters and caves for the night.

The postmaster nodded. But he was not yet prepared to offer employment. He still had some questions. For instance: Did Thompson know that four people had already applied for the job? Then tried it *and given up?*

"I will try it," the Norwegian said.

Did Thompson realize how brutally hard it would be? Just a few years ago a large group had set out with mules. The mules had frozen to death, and the party had limped on with their mail sacks. They had no food and almost died from hunger. After the ordeal they refused to go again. Other carriers had gone and been marooned all winter, starving.

"I will try it all the same," Thompson insisted.

But the postmaster had not finished with him. Did Thompson know about that very sturdy fellow named Absalom Woodward? He'd struggled with a load to Salt Lake City in 1851 but vanished 150 miles west of the town. They found him again in spring, this Absalom Woodward, his body pierced by Indian arrows.

Thompson said, "I will take the job."

"When?"

"As soon as you wish."

"Tomorrow morning?"

John Thompson nodded. "Yes," he said, squaring his broad frame. "Tomorrow morning."

II Into the Jaws of a Blizzard

HE SLEPT WELL that January night. The sky was pink with dawn when he came to the jumbled houses of Placerville. On the main street the log cabins and little wooden barracks still looked dark.

A lantern shone in the post office. A small group of miners stood outside, mumbling into their beards, as Thompson leaned his skis against the building and went in. Surprise! More people were inside, for word had spread about his trip. Thompson later learned that nine out of ten of the miners had bet that he would never come back alive. They felt he was doing a foolhardy, impossible thing. He would die in the January blizzards of the Sierras. No one would find him until spring. If he reached Genoa at all, it would be with a frozen limb which would have to be cut off, the miners said, fingering bowie knives in their belts.

But Thompson felt confident, and his faced showed it, too. He was ready to take on the 90-mile gamble. Living in Western America now, he was not one to make much of his Norwegian blood or to advertise his origins. Nor could he know that his countrymen—Fridtjof Nansen, Roald Amundsen, and others—would someday be famous Arctic explorers. Scandinavian men have always been able to bear the hardships and discomforts of the cold, and Thompson was no exception.

The Placerville postmaster weighed the black mail bag. Eighty pounds. Thompson quietly slung it across his shoulders.

"No jacket?" Mr. Thatcher wanted to know.

No jacket. It would be too cumbersome. It would slow him down. Thompson wore only a red miner's shirt, an ancient hat, a pair of sturdy pants, and high boots. For this first journey he also carried a pistol in a leather holster. Because he wanted to avoid extra weight, his food supply was slim, too—just a few biscuits, a piece of sausage, and some sun-dried meat strips that were called jerked beef. These provisions didn't seem much for a 180-pound man who would be in constant motion with a back-breaking load. Clearly, Thompson planned to reach his destination in a few days.

Outside the post office he took his skis and the long staff. Someone held out a bottle of whiskey. A swig? Thompson shook his head. He never touched the stuff. Another miner offered chewing tobacco. But the Norseman had no need for that, either. He could get along well without smoking. That was why the miners sometimes called him Holy John.

There were no more bets when John Thompson walked toward the snow at the upsweeping edge of town. There he took the wood planks from his shoulders and looked them over with pride. The tips curved beautifully, then reached a width of six inches. Toward the back his snowshoes tapered to four inches. Thompson's boots fitted in the center.

Several boys stared at him while he stuck his feet into the leather thongs. The rawhide strips would hold his toes down, and the heels of his boots sat against two nailed-on wood blocks.

Thompson bent down and fastened a strap around his ankles so that he wouldn't lose his runners if he fell. Placerville men wished him luck. They'd watch for his return. But their eyes seemed to say: *A dangerous journey. Gold panning is so much safer. Why isn't he mining like almost everyone else?*

Thompson had tried mining. A few years earlier, he'd panned in Placerville. He'd tried it at Coon Hollow, too, and stuck to it for two summers and winters. Few miners got rich there, and Thompson had never been one of the lucky ones. Whenever he arrived with his pan, a dozen other men came, too. He would go off to another lonely river, but so would the competition. Thompson didn't like fighting over claims, or cheating. He panned gold to pay for bacon, beans, and flapjacks. Thrifty as he was, he saved enough of the hard-won dust to buy the fields that made up his Putah Creek farm, but no more than that. Life in the 1850's was expensive. A candle cost a dollar. A pill—any pill—cost a dollar. An egg was three dollars, and a pair of shoes or a blanket would cost thirty times as much.

By noon the houses of Placerville were far below him. Left foot, right foot. His easy, rhythmic pace moved him past the next mining camp. Smithflat, they called it. The miners always claimed that Thompson wasn't interested in money. They were right. His heart hadn't been in mining. He just wasn't hungry enough for gold. People who knew him from the old country said his upbringing was at fault. A few years after his birth in April, 1827, near Tinn, Norway, his father had taken him into snow country, where only health and strength counted. Then, when he was old enough to understand, Thompson had been taught that wealth wasn't important.

He still believed that as an adult. In fact, he hadn't bothered to inquire about his carrier's wages. The postmaster had told Thompson that he'd be paid in Genoa, at the eastern foot of the Sierras. Another 80 miles.

The sky was clear that morning. By noon Thompson's eyes stung. He must have known that sun on snow could blind a man. It was painful business, this snow blindness. It could last for a day or longer. Thompson didn't want to risk it. One of his friends later said that Thompson blackened his face with coal to cut down the terrific glare. No one is sure whether he actually did it. Surely he pulled down the brim of his wide hat, which helped to protect his eyes from the glare. He scooped up some clean snow for a drink and munched a biscuit as he hurried on. Thompson was right so far about not bringing a jacket. The exercise kept him warm, and traveling light meant traveling fast. He carried no compass, either.

He followed the American River, which he knew well. Soon the ground turned upward again, and Thompson faced the mountain barrier. There was only one way to Genoa and Carson Valley—across the hard dragon spine of the Sierras. Steeper now. Sweating, Thompson clambered up in zigzags. Then he was in the pine forest where it seemed cooler.

To the summit! When he reached the crest, he could still see the river below him. From now on, there would be no people for many, many miles, no settlements of any kind. As the mountaintop dipped, Thompson bent into a slight crouch and flew down, holding the pole horizontally like a tightrope walker. The breeze was pleasant on his face. Down, to the tune of his rustling shirt! Down, to the bouncing of the sack on his back! He saw the white pillow of another hill coming toward him and darted upward as if on wings. The slope gradually stopped him.

It was a good way of braking. He climbed for another hour, then descended once more. This time he used the staff to slow down. Too much speed could mean a sudden bad fall, and that could be the end. But he'd done well so far.

Late in the afternoon the freshness began to leave him. He had a right to be tired: All day he had crossed gorges and canyons. He had traversed meadows. He had climbed and climbed, then made short downhill trips. Obviously, the route to Genoa meant more ups than downs. And the thick, ten-foot-long skis proved just too heavy. Thompson was sure he had made an error in using these weighty, overlong boards and decided to build lighter gear in the future. Right now his leg muscles throbbed with pain. His knees burned from the exertion. It was one thing to master a single Placerville hill, but quite another to fight six mountains. Besides, these peaks were three times as high as those in Norway. Thompson must have wondered about the challenge. Had he taken on more than he could handle? Would he be forced to return without completing the journey?

At least he didn't get lost. The river was still below him. He traveled in a straight line, keeping above a valley along which now runs State Highway 50. The sun was setting in the west, and he knew that Genoa was to the northeast.

Although Thompson did not keep a journal of his trip, he later reported some details to his employers. The first day he had managed to cover about 25 miles. The distance had exhausted him. The straps of his bag had bitten mercilessly into his shoulders. His shoulderblades were raw from the leather friction. The pain in his legs was scarcely bearable. His arms hurt from pulling his own body weight and the bag up so many crests. His eyes smarted from the glare. The inside of his chest ached

from breathing so hard. Thompson even resented the gun at his hip. Next time, he would leave this extra weight at home.

But would there be a next time?

At this point he could not have been sure. The sun had gone down within a span of minutes. All at once the mountain turned bitterly cold. Thompson hurried to find a cave for the night where he could be warm while he slept. There was none. He looked for a shielding rock. None. Finally he spied a hollow tree stump. He scooped out the snow and a layer of wet, rotten wood and found dry wood underneath. He dug into the nearby snow for some pine cones. From the trees he tore off some dead, dry twigs.

Now he removed his gloves and took matches wrapped in oil-cloth from his pocket. He lighted the cones. The fire caught. That night it would eat into the tree stump and keep him from freezing. He searched for pine boughs on which he could sleep.

Then it was night. Up here the stars stood out much more sharply than they did in the plains. Thompson pillowed his head against the postal bag and chewed a strip of beef jerky. He was at peace with the world. When he woke up it was still dark. The fire had long gone out. He later said he was so cold that he trembled, so he found a wide rock and performed a wild, lonely dance on it. He hopped from one leg to the other. He waved his arms. He beat his hands against his chest. Slowly he felt warmer.

To his surprise, though, the sky was gray, and as the sun rose, the granite mountains were more black than red. The wind told him that a storm would come. There was no time to lose. He had to get on, and fast. The trees stood out like so many black slashes against the lead-colored snow. But the snow cover had its advantages. Many of the rocks on Echo Summit were covered, so Thompson could skim across the surfaces. All the stones and bushes and underbrush were topped by snow. Perhaps he would not be delayed too much.

Once he saw bear tracks, although bears were rare in winter. He skied on as fast as he could. If he faced a bear, he would try to outrace it. But the track-dotted, speedy snow also held more immediate dangers. Shortly before noon he came to a deep mountain cleft. He listened: icy water ran deep under mounds of soft snow at the bottom. But a detour would surely take hours. So he decided to cross this snow and ice bridge. It was a mistake.

His skis suddenly dropped. One moment he was still in control and on a firm surface. The next moment he had broken through. A narrow river gaped below him. Deep down, rocks shone under the ice water. Fortunately Thompson's huge skis were already biting into the other river shore, and there was a leaning tree trunk he could grab. With his remaining strength he pulled himself all the way across. By then the sky was coal-dark.

The first snow fell in the afternoon. Thompson knew the perils. If he got stuck and suffered a frostbitten leg, if he lost his way, if he couldn't see where he was going and broke a leg, if he lost a runner, he would never reach Genoa. His food would run out, and he would die. Only a few miles beyond this spot, the Donner party had suffered a tragic fate ten years before. Thompson had read and reread the accounts about it. A blizzard had caused the loss of forty lives, and others of the party had survived by eating mules and dogs. In the end, they had even eaten dead humans.

Thompson couldn't stand being stranded. Yet no one could help him now as the snow swirled around his ears. He had to rely on himself.

He was on Ebbetts Pass when the blizzard hit in earnest. The snow hurtled down like millions of toothpicks, stabbing his eyes and pummeling his cheeks. Snow wedged into his gloves and pierced his shirt. Long ago he had lost sight of the 10,000-foot peak across the valley. He had to seek protection, but there were no cabins here. He hadn't seen human beings for more than 40 miles.

At last he found shelter under some overhanging rocks and made a fire. Hours later the Sierra skies showed another mood. The snowfall ceased as suddenly as it had begun. Thompson could see the stars again. The next morning—his third on the trail—the sun shone once more. It was mostly downhill into Carson Valley. Would he make Genoa by nightfall?

Thompson ate his remaining food and started off. Strength mysteriously was ebbing back into him as he got his second wind. He pushed on. He had always loved to travel in the mountains. Now he had a reason for his travel. The sack on his back was heavy, but he no longer felt it. He could make out a stretch of the Carson River far below. He pressed on; a little farther, the wide Carson Valley spread across the horizon. Far, far away he could spot the chimney smoke of Genoa. He would be welcome there. No one had to tell Thompson what mail meant to the miners. He knew from his own experience how they hungered for it. They were desperate for news.

Thompson poled hard. He skied a good line now, aiming straight for the peak that towered over Genoa. Mail for this camp could take months to arrive. All winter, in fact. Thompson had done it in three days. He had won.

Thompson emerged just below Genoa Peak. The town rested at the foot of the steep mountain. In the clear, late-afternoon light, he could see the houses beneath him and the stockade which the Mormons had built. He could look into the streets.

Then he was in the pines, stabbing his pole into the snow for more speed. He swept past boulders. He was borne upward in flight. He sailed down and down. He had never known such joy.

People in town were puzzled at the sight of the approaching dot. At first they were not sure what it was. They rushed out of saloons. They left their forges and workbenches. They raced on their horses toward the descending man. When Thompson sped into Genoa he was surrounded by a crowd. They would talk and write a long time about the event.

Mr. S. A. Kinney, the postmaster, invited Thompson to dinner and let him sleep in the back of the post office. Of course the carrier forgot to ask Mr. Kinney about his wages. Instead he wanted to know if there was any mail for Placerville.

Plenty of mail. For Sacramento, too.

The return trip was easier because it went more downhill. Thompson needed only two days to reach his starting point. Again men saw him as he flitted past rocky crags and stormed out of trees. Hadn't they made bets?

Now they ran into the streets, pointing, yelling, cheering. One miner rang the church bells. Another shot a rifle into the sky. They were saluting him. Tumult reigned in Placerville, California. Several women had tears of joy in their eyes.

John A. Thompson had made it.

Snowshoe Thompson.

A postal route was born with this historic January trip. But it was only the beginning. Thompson's real feats, his life-saving deeds, and his great sacrifices for others were still to come.

III Voyages

OF COURSE, John Thompson had much in his favor.

He was born on April 30, 1827, in a country which extends beyond the Arctic Circle. Even in the south of Norway, where John was brought up, the snows linger until April, and most of the year the wind blows through broad-shouldered mountains. It is made for hardy people.

John's parents were farmers. This proved to be good preparation, too. John's mother and stepfather led no easy lives; in fact, no one did in Telemark County. A rugged day's work was the rule for everyone. Even six-year-olds had to help at home, and at the age of eight, John already had his chores in the fields and gardens. Scandinavian farm families do not coddle their children, and John's older brother, Torstein, helped with the plowing, sowing, and harvesting, while his stepsister, Tina, washed dishes and lent a hand to clean house and pick fruit.

Of course there was no motorized farm machinery in those days. Even a wagon and horse were something special. So John quickly developed muscles as a boy. The schools he attended were miles away. At that time children had never heard of school buses, for such luxuries didn't exist yet. In Upper Tinn, Telemark, you *walked.* This put a ruddy color into John's cheeks, and the summer sun bleached his beautiful fair hair.

As a vacation treat the family visited the coast one summer. John's father knew many of the wild ocean inlets, which are called fjords, and John was stunned by rocks that shot up as straight as the masts of the big ships at sea, only much, much higher. They were blunt, awesome rocks, overlooking the dark blue of the water and blotting out the light-blue summer sky. John learned that a view such as this could be the greatest thrill in the world. Scenery meant more than riches.

In winter John learned all about handling the family sleigh, which carried milk and other farm products to market in the nearest two Norwegian towns, Prestijeld and Guasta. Older people used sleighs for winter transportation. But skiing was the best way to get from place to place for everyone else. In winter, therefore, John sped to school on skis. The Telemark postmen came on skis; the doctor made his calls on skis; neighbors visited on skis; and all the healthy, robust Norwegian families went to church on skis. Indeed, the Telemark mountains became the cradle of skiing in Europe. The first ski bindings were invented there, and the first real ski turns were made there. Ski racing started there. The best jumpers came from this region.

But farming was poor in Telemark County, and many families —including John's folks—dreamed of better soil and more land. One day in 1837 something happened that was to change John's life.

Two friends arrived at the farm on their long, upcurved boards. They were Ole and Ansten Nattestad, and they'd skied to Upper Tinn all the way from the east coast of Norway, up one mountain and down the next. Heavily loaded with knapsacks, the two young men were on their way to Oslo. "We're going to America!" they announced.

John was much impressed.

To *America* on skis?

No, the ten-year-old was told. Only to the boat on skis!

The Nattestads promised to write. And they did. They'd settled in the American Midwest. Land was good and plentiful, and more people would be needed to farm it. Almost right away, John's elders were preparing for their own trip to America. This was in the boys' favor, too. So John learned that sometimes in life it is worth moving, and that it is good to take the risks of a long journey. His pioneering spirit was born.

The Torsteinsons, as the family called themselves, planned with care. They wrote letters to America and sought out people who'd been there. What sort of clothes were needed? Which tools should they take? What kind of foods were scarce across the sea? How much money should they have for their overland trip? They got all the answers from the Nattestad boys and from others in the Norwegian colony. The Torsteinsons picked all the items which they had to take with them and then sold their Upper Tinn farm. Finally, they bought the ship's ticket on the *Engiheden,* which, tightly packed, sailed from Oslo. The departure must have been a heart-thumping event for the blue-eyed boy and his brother and sister. Ocean travel! A real ship! A new, unknown land!

John and his folks joined the Nattestads in La Salle County, Illinois, then moved to an old Missouri farm in 1838. The Torsteinsons stayed there until John was a husky, tall boy of fourteen. Although they didn't get around to skiing, John was almost always outdoors, working the fields, building and repairing a house, sheds, or fences, setting traps for quail and prairie chickens and wild turkeys. His folks gave a good example of seeing work as a joy and not a torture. The man of the house was experienced with his hands, like most Scandinavians, and John's mother was a thrifty woman.

In 1841 much of the Norwegian colony left for Iowa, and so did the Torsteinsons. A few years later they once more returned to Illinois. John grew into a man who could skillfully handle a hammer, a chisel, and a saw and who didn't mind working in the fields with only the sky and the wide-angled earth for company. He was not one to speak much about the miles he covered or the crops he helped bring in. He wasn't a talker, anyway.

But excitement gripped him all the same when he heard, in 1849, about the great opportunities in California. Gold had been found at Sutter's Mill, and there were the true stories of men who after only a few months had accumulated enough wealth to buy themselves the best possible California ranchland. Everything grew much faster out on the West Coast, John had heard. Some crops could be harvested several times a year, and the country was beyond compare for cattle breeding and fruit growing. All through the next fifteen months the stories flew in thick and fast, and most able-bodied young men were heading for California.

So the day came when John, too, had to say good-bye to his family. He was twenty-four years old now, slim and wiry and strong, and burning with the sense of adventure. Before they parted, his mother said, "All right, son, go west. Perhaps there's something more out there. Something that only *you* can do." John would always remember those words.

After embracing his mother and taking leave of the rest of his family, the adventurous Norwegian rode to St. Louis, where most of the travelers gathered. He changed his name from Jon Torsteinson to John Thompson because it would be easier to pronounce.

From St. Louis it was some 2,000 miles to the West Coast. The grinding trail led to Kansas City, St. Joseph, over the flat, vast land to Fort Kearney, and finally along the North Platte River to the Mormon country in the West. Families made the journey in canvas-topped farm wagons, pulled by oxen. The wagons screeched and squeaked and rattled, yet they covered no more than 12 to 20 miles a day. Ninety days of continuous travel! Thompson, being alone and on horseback, could move faster. But it was still too slow for him. What an immense continent America was!

Only healthy people could survive the crossing, and Thompson saw hundreds die on the way. Families ran out of food, and in the deserts water was scarce. Some older folks were just not strong enough to stand the rigors, and even young men—who hailed from European or Eastern American cities—fell apart on the trek. Graves seemed to be everywhere.

Some immigrants lost their way or were killed by Indians or just gave up somewhere between St. Louis and Salt Lake City. Nothing like that happened to Thompson, according to the letters he sent home. And it wasn't in his character to give up. He merely described the trip as dusty and tedious. Thompson didn't mind the thirst and the bad water and sleeping outdoors on the ground and riding with the rain whipping his face. Nor did it cause him pain to go hungry for a while. Only the endless country bored him. Plains, plains, plains as far as the eye could see!

At last, weeks later, there was the wavy line of the Rocky Mountains. It grew in size. Thompson rode closer. He could take a deep breath. When he reached the eastern foothills of the Sierra Nevadas, he was downright excited. Perhaps he would remain right in this country; perhaps there was no need to travel all the way to the West Coast. In Placerville, then called Hangtown, on the western side of the Sierras, Thompson met up with some miners. "Why don't you stay here?" they said. "There's plenty of gold in them rivers."

Thompson bought a gold pan and learned to wash out the precious metal. He got himself a rocker to separate the gravel from the gold. For several months he shook the rocker at Coon Hollow and Kelsey's Diggings. Perhaps he didn't move along the rivers fast enough because he wasn't smitten with real gold fever; perhaps competition was too strong and there wasn't enough gold left in the rivers to go around. Besides, by 1854 the time had come when men burrowed through the earth, and much of the better mining was done for wages in deep tunnels and shafts. Thompson liked the sky and fresh air too much; subterranean mining just wasn't for him. When more of the river gold gave out, Thompson went back to his old love—farming. Then early in 1856 he at last found his real profession of carrying the mails.

His mail run took shape, applauded by all. Placerville to Genoa on skis. Genoa to Placerville. And all camps in between. He had never been so happy before, and on every trip he must have felt as if he were again a boy in Telemark. Snowshoe Thompson propelled himself forward with his long pole, his skis cutting ribbons into the white land.

He was bothered by only one problem. Did he really need 25-pound gear? The skis were just too heavy, making each climb uncomfortable and slowing him down besides. After some weeks he noticed another thing. His long skis proved difficult to handle amid the thick trees. True, overlong, overheavy runners meant speed and steadiness on the down-the-hill portions, but the same devices were impossible everywhere else. And much of this Sierra wilderness required quick reactions and light equipment. So at the first opportunity Thompson built himself another, lighter pair. This time he avoided green oak but used spruce instead. This wood proved more flexible. He didn't need a length of ten feet. Seven and a half was sufficient. Again he stuck the tips into a bucket of hot water, which allowed bending. Again he fixed himself a pair of rawhide bindings.

He noticed the difference at once. It was almost as if he had wings under his feet. He could fly! In the flat Carson Valley he strove for better rhythm in gliding. At every mile, his right-foot-left-foot tempo got better. It became as natural as a person's stride on dry ground. Soon each step flowed, dreamlike. He improved his downhill stance, too, his legs wide apart for stability, the pole balanced crosswise. He seldom fell, and the heavy postal bag on his back no longer pinched or rubbed him.

All that winter he conquered Ebbetts Pass and Carson Pass and the whole length of pine-rimmed Lake Tahoe. At the Placerville Hotel, at Strawberry Station in Woodfords, at Markleeville, at the tiny Genoa post office and the Genoa stockade, at the

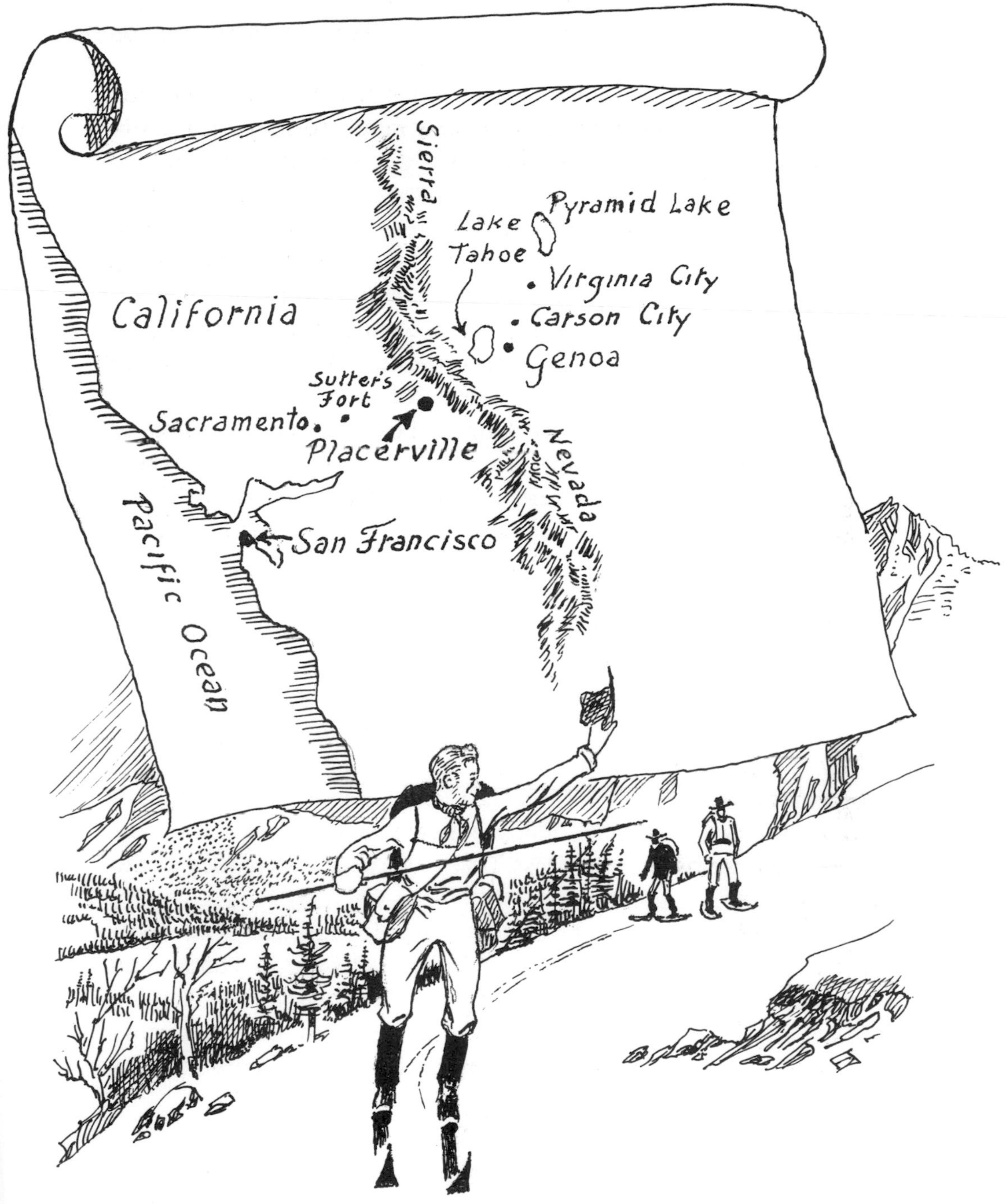

Sierra
Nevada
Pyramid Lake
Lake
Tahoe
Virginia City
Carson City
Genoa
California
Sutter's
Fort
Sacramento
Placerville
San Francisco
Pacific Ocean

St. Charles Hotel in Carson City—everywhere letters awaited him. They had stamps on them, just as mail does now. But there were no envelopes at that time; a letter was merely a folded sheet, sealed with wax.

Soon he began to carry packages as well; merchants who owned stores on both sides of the snow-blocked mountains would ask Thompson if he minded taking boxes with warm socks, sorely needed by the miners. Apart from the mail, he transported matches, writing paper, and small Bibles. Before the spring thaw there would be seeds of all kinds.

No one mocked him any longer. No one expected him to freeze to death in the snow caves en route. One day he found himself in Woodfords, where the little dry-goods store hadn't found enough sales for its miner's boots. The store owner waved to Snowshoe Thompson. "How about taking a shipment to Virginia City?"

Thompson nodded, and they quickly agreed on the shipping rate.

There were enough boots for three carriers, though, and Thompson stalked from one prospector's shack to the next. Any men willing to help?

No one dared to come. At last, on his second trip around, he found two rough-and-ready types who'd heard about the Norwegian's speed and fitness. They were sure that they could match both.

The men owned webbed snowshoes. It was true that other carriers before Thompson—notably Fred Bishop in 1853—had managed to cross the Sierras that way. Webbed gear was much in use in Canada at the time, and it at least kept one from sinking into the snow. Maybe they'd do better than Thompson's skis for climbing, the men said. And they might surprise him downhill, too. "Virginia City?" they said in unison. "Sixty miles? That ain't nothing!"

"Come on then," Thompson said quietly.

"We'll keep up!" And they kept their word as Thompson took the steep route up the flanks of Job's Peak. Five thousand feet. Six thousand. Still they climbed. Seven thousand above sea level. Eight. But then it went downhill. Thompson, with package heaped upon package strapped on his back, soared on his skis. He was doing almost a mile a minute. But the two others, already much more exhausted from the unaccustomed climb than Thompson, had to rest before the descent. Then they clumsily padded downhill on their oval, leather webbed snowshoes.

They couldn't make any time at all. Thompson waited for them in good humor. The two miners were very slow. The sweat ran down their faces when they came in sight. It continued in this way for a full downhill day; Thompson shooting ahead, then waiting.

Carson Valley was already in sight in all its magnificent width. At least they couldn't get lost. Thompson gave them instructions to head straight down to the road, then turn north on it toward Carson City, then northeast toward Virginia City,

Thompson himself delivered the boots in Virginia City by the next night and picked up a load of mail for Woodfords and other points. The two miners were just below Genoa when Thompson encountered them on the snow-covered road. They'd done 30 miles in three days. And they were awfully tired.

"How much farther?" they wanted to know.

"Another thirty miles," Thompson said.

The two porters looked at each other and, without saying another word, plodded on, bent by their load.

Thompson continued his way to Woodfords.

Somewhere in the winter landscape his mother's words must have come back to him. He had found the right occupation out west.

IV A Man with Frozen Feet

THOMPSON'S MOTHER would have been proud of her son John in the Middle West if she'd still been alive. *Perhaps there's something more out there. Something that only you can do.*

He pulled beautifully through his first winter as a long-distance mail carrier. He spent the summer and fall on his farm near Sacramento. Now, just before Christmas, 1856, he attacked post office duties with renewed vigor. People had no doubts that he would make it, through gales and in subzero weather. After the first snows fell, he proved his mettle in other ways, too. One snowy afternoon Snowshoe Thompson got to Strawberry Station with his heavy pouch. After he'd unloaded part of his mail, the postmaster drew him aside. It seemed that early in the day three prospectors in search of minerals had started toward the rocky crest without snowshoes of any kind. Travel led through deep snow, and the men had promised to report back at the post office. But they hadn't returned. "A foolhardy lot," the postmaster said. "But someone has to go after them and see what happened."

Thompson inquired about the prospectors' direction. Although it was blowing, the tracks of the three men were still faintly visible in the snow, and the Norwegian followed them. At first the men had had fairly firm ground under their feet. But after a few miles Thompson spied deep holes in the snow. So the prospectors had broken through. Still, they had gone on. Thompson battled upward through the drifts. Five miles. Seven. Nine.

Finally he saw them. They were bogged down in the wet whiteness to their armpits. They'd become so feeble that they could go neither forward nor backward. They were stuck and might have perished if help hadn't come.

Thompson selected the weakest of the three men. "Plant your feet on the back of my skis," Thompson told him. "And hold on to my chest!"

Trembling, the miner grappled his way out of the hole, then mounted just behind Thompson's heels. Asking the others to wait—under no circumstances must they use up the rest of their strength or wander away—Thompson now pushed off with the passenger in back of him. The downhill ride was fast enough, and there was sufficient room for the stranded man's boots behind Thompson. They got down to Strawberry Station in about half an hour, to the postmaster's amazement. Then Thompson set out for the two other prospectors, bringing them down one at a time.

In Carson Valley they would talk about Thompson for a long time to come. In the saloons and the rickety hotels and the miner's shacks Snowshoe Thompson's name came up again and again. Yet Thompson sought no publicity for his deeds, and he never boasted about his strength. He didn't go to the taverns himself. Brook water or throat-mellow snow was enough drink

for him. And while present-day skiers in the modernistic warming houses and the ski lodges around Lake Tahoe must stuff themselves with enormous meals, Thompson could get along on very little food. He never varied his diet of jerked beef or dry sausage and biscuits or crackers. After all, he knew pretty well the time he would reach the next town, where a warm meal awaited him. He had his schedule, and he stuck to it.

Some of the stranded people he encountered in lonely cabins had no such luck. One winter day Thompson was passing a tiny shack that lay on his route. Someone called out to him, and Thompson went up close. He saw a man gaunt from hunger, bones sticking out from his skull. "I'm lost," the stranger said.

Thompson listened to his story. It seems that this Californian had tried desperately to reach a town from the little shack, where he had taken shelter during a storm. The man had set out every morning in the hope of finding his way. And every night he returned to the cabin, unable to get his bearings anywhere en route. Thompson learned that the helpless Californian had floundered like this for four days. He didn't know one mountain from another. He didn't know anything about rock formations or trees, and he couldn't read the direction from the stars.

"Tell me which valley you got to," Thompson said.

The man described it.

"That was Hope Valley," Thompson said. "Did you see a river going down out of the mountains?"

"Yep, I saw one. I reckon it was the American River."

Thompson shook his blond head. "You saw the main branch of the Carson River. Six miles down that would have taken you to Carson City."

The man rubbed his stubbled cheeks. While the two people

warmed themselves inside the shanty, Thompson learned the rest of the fellow's story. For four days he had had nothing to eat but a few potatoes he'd found in the cabin. He had cooked these potatoes, but now they were all gone. If Thompson hadn't come to help him get out of the wilderness, he would probably have starved to death. Even with Thompson's meager food supplies, the man had barely enough strength left to reach Carson City now. But he made it.

Thompson's own endurance was soon put to a test, too. A few days before Christmas, 1856, he was on his way from Placerville to Woodfords and Genoa. He felt well rested and was in a fine fettle. The blunt 10,000-foot-high Monument Peak was already in sight when Thompson paused on his skis and shifted his pouch. He must have felt at peace with the world; the tree sap smelled sweet, and his blood pulsed warmly from the long hours of motion. He skied on. In Lake Valley the forest was quiet. Below, equally silent, Lake Tahoe glinted up through the trees. Thompson would be in Genoa—his final destination—in the afternoon of the next day.

Thompson stabbed his man-sized pole into the snow, and before darkness set in, he took the straightest possible ski line through the sloping land. He didn't know it yet, but if he had veered by a few miles west or east, destiny might have changed another man's life. The other man might have died. As it happened that night, Thompson pointed his skis past a little log shanty. During summer it served as a small trading post, but now it seemed as still in the wintry landscape as the rising moon. Thompson wondered if he should rest here for an hour or so. Should he get a little sleep? No, there wouldn't be time; the people were expecting their mail at noon the next day, and he couldn't keep them waiting.

But he was hungry. It would be good to eat his provisions under a real roof. He knew that cabins were always kept open during the winter for travelers who might chance by in a blizzard. Thompson skied up closer to the little log hut, tempted to take a look inside. No tracks at all. No footsteps. No sign of life—only masses of snow blocking the lower part of the door.

John Thompson took off his runners. His beef jerky would taste good beside a fire. He clapped his skis together; then he heard a human voice.

Inside the hut someone was groaning.

Thompson caught his breath. He listened. Through the night there came again a sob of pain.

Using the tips of his skis, the Scandinavian mailman shoveled the snow from the door, then pushed it inward. The moonlight illuminated a figure resting on a thin layer of hay. The man had no blanket; although the temperature in the cabin must have been below zero, there was no fire in the fireplace. Thompson also noticed that the fellow's boots were off. The bearded face was drawn with pain.

Thompson drew closer. "What's your name?"

"James Sisson," the man moaned.

"You have an ax, James Sisson?"

"An ax? Why?"

"To make a fire for you," Thompson explained gently.

Sisson pointed to a corner. Snowshoe Thompson took out a match and struck it. In the brief flare he saw the ax gleam on the ground. Suddenly Sisson spoke: "Don't dull that ax!"

Thompson carried it toward the door, ready to cut some wood

outside. "Don't dull it none!" Sisson called after him again. "Be careful of the rocks!"

Snowshoe Thompson returned with an armful of logs and kindling. He quickly made a fire, and when it burned, Sisson inquired again about the ax. Was it still sharp?

"Why?" Thompson said.

"Need it," Sisson croaked. "Tomorrow." In the growing brightness of the fireplace, the old man pulled up his dirt-caked trousers legs and pointed to his feet. For the first time, Thompson understood.

Sisson's legs were purple to the knees. Then Sisson explained it. He had come here twelve chilly days ago. During the first four days his feet had frozen onto his boots. Then he found a match, lighted a fire, and thus managed to get off his boots. Eventually the fire had gone out, but Sisson had grown too weak to light it again. In great pain, unable to crawl out for more wood, he had writhed here for eight more days while the wind and snow hammered against the cabin. Eight days of torture. Tomorrow would be the last day, he said. Tomorrow he'd finally cut off his frozen legs. If he didn't do it, he'd surely die of gangrene.

Sisson, a trapper, had already decided on the details. He said he would twist some baling rope with a stick around his knees. The rope would serve as a tourniquet to stop the blood flow while he operated on himself.

Thompson listened patiently, then began to talk about the dangers of an amputation. Maybe it wasn't necessary, Thompson said. In any case, it wouldn't be clean here. Besides, too much blood would be lost, even with a rope. And what's more, was Sisson strong enough for all this? What had he eaten during the twelve days?

Thompson saw the torn-open sack, which had been the man's only food. Sisson had hoped to find more when he stumbled into the shanty during a storm, but that was all there was. It later turned out that Indians had burglarized the cabin. "I'm starving!" Sisson mumbled.

Thompson didn't have to think long. He still had the piece of dried beef. True, he'd traveled a whole afternoon and half the night without a bite, and he himself hungered for it now. But Sisson needed it far more. The visitor sliced the meat for the other man. And Sisson gratefully wolfed down each morsel.

"I will bring more," Thompson promised. "And help."

The bearded trapper looked up. He shook his head. "No one can buck this snow."

"With skis, I can make it to Genoa."

"You won't come back," Sisson predicted.

Thompson quietly reassured the man. Adding action to his words, he fetched more wood. He put some logs into the fire and stacked another bundle near the prone man. "When I return, I will take you away from here." In his calmly authoritative way, Thompson persuaded the ailing trapper not to touch the ax, and not to think of amputations, but to wait.

Outside, the Norwegian pushed his hat a little deeper onto his head. He would have to ski faster than usual.

Much faster. A man's life was at stake.

V Endurance

SNOWSHOE THOMPSON pushed himself hard through the sleepless night. His skis sliced the snow without a pause, left foot, right foot, legs slightly bent, keeping on the level. At the bottom of Monument Peak, where modern skiers would wait for the big aerial tramways to take them up a hundred years later, Thompson did not halt either, but sped on, avoiding the steep slopes. He crossed over from the California side to Nevada's south shore of Lake Tahoe, which is now a city of gambling casinos. Instead of the neon-lit skyscrapers, only a few desolate cabins huddled there. Eight-cylinder cars today blast uphill on Highway 19, across Daggett Pass, with nary a modern skier considering climbing more than 10 feet. Thompson pushed himself up a grade that rises some 1,000 feet. His stomach was empty, but his mind was clear, despite the lack of sleep. Unlike present-day skiers on the Sierras, Thompson was used to walking and demanded nothing more than a journey such as this. He would have never dreamed that the region would someday be covered by ski lifts of every description. Nor would today's average skier match Thompson's downhill achievements. Sisson's plight drove Thompson to 60-mile downhill speeds, to incredible jumps.

Despite the long hours with Sisson, Snowshoe Thompson got to Genoa on schedule, shortly after noon. He at once disposed of his Placerville mail at the Genoa post office and then strove to find help.

It was anything but easy. Men had their own business to take care of just then. They had little time to spare, and certainly not for a James Sisson, whom they didn't know. The Genoa people had claims to stake and mining shifts to work, and the tradesmen had their eyes on the customer's gold dust. Yet wherever the tall, blond mail carrier turned up in town—at Mr. Kinney's post office, in the forges and offices, in the shacks of the workmen—faces would now light up at the sight of his blue eyes. Snowshoe Thompson! An emergency? A necessary errand? If the Norwegian reckoned that he required help, why, then they would help him. Thompson himself later recalled the people who joined him in the mission. Not all the names, and not the first names, but enough for history, anyhow. Thompson was joined by W. B. Wade, Harris, Jacobs, and two other old Genoa settlers. "Take all the tools and blankets you can," they were told. "We will have to build a sled!"

At least one of the men knew how to ski a little, and two of them were strong enough to learn it. So the Scandinavian borrowed a few pairs of skis from friends, and some webbed snowshoes for two of the rescuers. The men also packed more food, and whereas Thompson wore only a jacket and a shirt, his partners had on thick, clumsy coats. But on the way up there was trouble right away. Several of the men slipped backward just as Thompson had done when he had learned all over. They fumbled on the hill, getting their boards crossed. They didn't know where to plant the long pole. Then, whenever the trail led downward, the newly minted skiers got scared and leaned their shoulders back. So they fell, and Thompson had to pull them out of the snow because novices don't know how to get up again. All the way to Lake Valley, Thompson had to give lessons so that his crew would make better time. He did this with good humor, never raising his voice, never commanding. Not that ski instruction was anything new to Snowshoe Thompson. During these first seasons he had already made a name for himself as a teacher in the mining camps. Whenever he turned up, Thompson was surrounded by youngsters, some of whom had nothing but barrel staves. What's more, Thompson's countrymen had teaching in their blood. While our hero was instructing in the Sierra Nevadas, other Norwegians taught the Canadians to ski and introduced this kind of travel in such far-flung earth corners as New Zealand.

Although Thompson was slowed down by the beginners and by the Genoa men on webbed snowshoes, the party reached Sisson's cabin by evening.

The trapper just couldn't believe it. He wept with joy. He even held up his frozen legs to show he hadn't touched them with the ax after all. Sisson had a lot of praise for Thompson, who was awake for a second night and who now helped the others construct a handsled. They wanted a solid one, which took several hours of hammering. Then one of the Genoa fellows cooked a crude meal for all of them, and though he was still in great pain, Sisson ate his fill with the rescuers. Afterward, one of Thompson's companions pulled out a tobacco pouch and some thin paper. He rolled himself a cigarette before the long journey. Would Thompson want to smoke? The Norwegian thanked the man and refused.

Toward dawn they were ready to go. Thompson opened the door, and they carried the blanket-covered Sisson outside, placing him onto the homemade toboggan.

A surprise awaited them. In addition to about eight feet of snow on the ground, a fresh two feet had fallen during the night. This made travel extremely difficult, for the sled sank deeply into the white powder. Thompson, on his skis, led the way, pulling and tugging the rope attached to the sled. Two other men were behind him, on shorter skis, to drag the load. And three more fellows were pushing from behind with all their strength. The flat stretches were bad enough, but the climb over the mountain pass proved even tougher. Here they fought the man-sized quicksandlike drifts. At each step, their first-aid vehicle got stuck deeper, but they plodded upward, inch by inch. Thompson's companions were cursing, then silent, then cursing again. They made only a brief nighttime stop and pressed on. On the final downhill journey from Genoa Peak, matters improved for the rescuers. The sled was running better. At last the exhausted men saw wisps of smoke in the valley, then the bare chestnut trees of Genoa. Under the brow of Genoa Peak there was less snow. Then the cover hardened, so they made the remaining descent at a fine clip.

In Genoa it was morning. Snowshoe Thompson had battled a third night without real sleep. But according to eyewitnesses, his strength still had not dwindled.

It was Thompson who sought out Dr. Luce, the physician in the mountain community.

The patient was still alive. But Dr. Luce agreed that his legs would have to be amputated.

The doctor saw only one problem. Sisson was too weak to stand the operation without anesthesia. Dr. Luce needed chloroform before he could amputate.

The men wanted to know where the drug could be obtained.

Where? The nearest place was Sacramento, which is now the California capital. And Sacramento lay hours beyond Placerville, which was 90 snow-blocked miles from Genoa! Of all the men in the physician's office—in fact, of all the men in Genoa at that very instant—only one person would be able to cross the Sierras safely, quickly, reach the supply house, and bring back chloroform.

It was Snowshoe Thompson, of course. It was the mail carrier they had mocked a year earlier. Thompson stood before them, eyes red-rimmed from the three hard nights without sleep. They didn't even have to ask him whether he would do it. He just nodded and said he would go. But was he still strong enough? Yes, he was. Willingly, he also planned the details: from Placerville he would use a horse to the railroad station in Folsom, California, then take a train to Sacramento. Where would he sleep? On the train, of course. He would return to Genoa in the same manner—by train, by horse, then on skis.

But Dr. Luce, Wade, Harris, Jacobs, and the others still had their doubts. It seemed impossible that Snowshoe Thompson would want to undertake such a grueling journey. Or would he really?

Dan De Quille, a famous newspaperman of the period, who eventually interviewed eyewitnesses, tells us what happened next. In fact, De Quille wrote it all down for us in the *Territorial*

Enterprise: "As Snowshoe Thompson never did things by halves, he at once set out across the Sierras in order to get the required drug. Finally, the long-delayed operation was performed. So modest was Thompson that what others called great feats, did not appear so to him."

As for Sisson, he survived the operation. At a time in the history of the West when men shot their best friends, Thompson had saved the life of a total stranger.

VI Nature's Dangers

DURING MOST OF HIS JOURNEYS Thompson faced the wintry wilderness alone. The deeper and longer he pushed into the Sierra Nevadas with his skis, the more he liked it. Black pouch on his back, he loved to be alone with his thoughts and with the mountains. Contrary to modern skiers, who enjoy the sport only in the company of many others, Snowshoe Thompson was perfectly happy on his own. He relished the elbowroom of the high country. He lived for the three to five days when he could cut his solitary arcs through the whiteness. He waited for the moment when he could take yet another bird's-eye view of a river's thin silver band far below or when, above the brow of a peak, the California sky suddenly opened up, wide, wide in all its blueness. Season after season, he was to ski between the tiny mountain communities, and despite the hardships, he liked each day a little better.

Yet people kept asking him: Wasn't he bored? Wasn't it monotonous to see nothing but trees and rocks and snow? Thompson would silently shake his head in reply. He was never one for talking, except during an emergency. But to him, and to those who have learned to appreciate the outdoors in winter, nature is never the same from day to day. It changes constantly. If you have skied for a long time, you will find this easy to understand.

Take the snow. Thompson skied through soft, billowing, winglike snow up to his hips. He skied across firm snow which the wind had shaped into a bumpy surface. He skied through snow that had hardened from dropping temperatures, and he sometimes guided his ten-foot-long boards across ice that made crunching, screeching noises. After it got warm, or after a rain, the snow could become as wet and sticky as fresh cement, which made turning difficult and would require a lot of muscle power even for the straight, level runs. On other occasions, only the top inch of the snow surface melted, and this meant speedy skiing.

Thompson skied under a constantly changing sky. Clouds could suddenly dot the heavens before and above him, clouds as white as the snow itself, gray clouds, black clouds, mauve clouds, or the red clouds at dawn. The snow changed from a diamond sparkle under the sun to the blue of late afternoon to the grayest and the blackest hues before a storm. When the mountain sun blazed in spring and the light was right, the snow could be as brightly golden as honey. There were hundreds of different rock formations, each unlike the next. In the Sierras rocks can fall away as straight as a building or just like beams hanging over a deep drop. On Thompson's route there were boulders more massive than half a dozen barns topping one another and formations that resembled dragons and owls and Gothic churches.

Sometimes Thompson would play a game with himself. He would estimate his altitude from the rock strata. He could tell whether he was about 6,000 feet above sea level by the browns of sandstone or whether he faced a gleaming red granite that could be found only at 10,000 feet. Trees would give Thompson similar clues; at from 6,000 to 8,000 feet he found the ponderosa pine, with its thick trunks and open cones. There were other kinds of pine; it stirred his mind to tell them apart not only because they grew on different elevations but also from the sheer smell. The ponderosa pine, for instance, has a bark that smells like vanilla. And whether the branches drooped with snow or not, Thompson could always distinguish the lodge pole pine. Its trunks were much thinner, and it grew much higher up. The presence of spruce told Thompson how high he was, and so did certain fir trees, the hemlock, and above 10,000 feet, the Alpine firs. Trees gave him still additional information. He could guess from them whether he found himself north or south. He was also guided by the moss on the tree bark, for moss always grows on the north side of a tree.

But he liked it best above timberline. No obstacle blocked his view then, and his eyes could roam and roam. Naturally, Thompson varied his route, too. He was always seeking shortcuts so he could deliver his letters faster, and he was seeking fresh vistas as well. As he made trip after trip between Placerville and Genoa, between Genoa and Woodfords, and between Strawberry Station and Carson City, he would seek new approaches.

When the weather was good, he would sometimes follow the steepest possible slant, which meant the hardest one but also—as the crow flies—the shortest. Soon he knew each river, each valley, and each quaking-aspen-covered canyon in the area. The beauty of the sights never stopped satisfying him.

Thompson's life also became more suspenseful because he switched from daytime travel to night journeys. He preferred the night when the sun shone too brightly during the day. Because of the heat, the snow would then stick to his runners, and it proved difficult to get ahead fast enough on the mushy ground. So before noon he would hole up somewhere, usually under some rocks or in a snow cave, and wait to travel again after the sun disappeared behind the mountains. At night it was colder, even in spring, and the frozen snow allowed him to gain all the speed necessary to be on schedule.

He loved to ski with the moon showing the way. The snows reflected the light beautifully. Although it was night, every contour of the country stood out; moving along far above the towns, Thompson would find the atmosphere as clear as in a desert. No mining or smelter smoke and no dust clouded the nights, so each star pierced the sky with incredible sharpness. And way above Thompson the Milky Way would shine, too!

He never needed a compass. In clear weather the North Star was enough for guidance. Not once did Thompson get lost. He had too much travel wisdom for that, and he knew his mountain world too well. But during one particular trip he was severely tested. He'd slept through the day, and he was eager to get ahead before his sturdy pocket watch showed midnight. Toward eleven o'clock it clouded up for a late spring storm. In a jiffy the moon was blotted out and the North Star and the Big Dipper vanished behind the snow that was balling up in the air. Suddenly, as it sometimes happens in spring, tons of spring snow began to fall. Another man might have gone on all the same, battling the elements, and perhaps lost his way. But Thompson found an overhanging rock and for once stayed put. He had hardly strayed from his route. While the snow gusted and whistled before him there was no point in going farther. Thompson crouched in the shelter for five hours. Then, just as suddenly as they had come, the last clouds tore to shreds and were blown away by the wind. The final night hours—and a clear sky—had come again. The North Star, the Big Dipper, Orion, and Andromeda once more became his compass needles.

In the depth of winter and in spring he would also share the mountains with every kind of animal. So he was really not all alone, and his companions changed with the season and the clock. After a freeze was over, for instance, the raccoons emerged from their quarters. Thompson shared the nights with these harmless mammals. Sometimes he would see only their thinnish tracks, which looked a little like a child's handprints. At other times Thompson would suddenly catch sight of their thick gray furs that reach down all the way to their small toes. One night he skied silently around a corner in the moonlight, and three coons stared at him out of their dark, black-masked eyes. He didn't bother them, and they didn't bother him. He silently skied up and down the mounds of woodchucks having their winter sleep, and the dainty tracks of squirrels and chipmunks. He could tell from the distance between the tracks whether the animals had walked or run.

After his first few years on his mail route, Thompson did not carry a gun. He had done so only during the initial few trips. "A gun would slow me down," he answered when asked about it. But what about Indians? his friends wanted to know. What if he encountered a dangerous tribe? Thompson was sure that on a downhill stretch he could outrace their arrows, for he knew of no Indians in the Sierras who skied. And didn't he fear the mountain lions and bears? For a reply, Thompson would shrug his broad shoulders, and it was true that during all his years outdoors he was never attacked by the grizzlies or mountain lions, although he saw many of their tracks.

But one harrowing day in 1857 he was face to face with dangerous animals. He had skied down a part of Hope Valley when he spied, in the middle of his trail, a pack of lean, ugly-looking timber wolves.

Thompson stopped. Six wolves measured him across a half-buried animal carcass in the snow. They were starved. In the presence of a human being, they stopped chewing and snarled. Their green eyes were red with viciousness. Thompson knew that hungry timber wolves could tear a human being to pieces. Should he turn back the way he'd come? Impossible! If he fled, they'd pursue him uphill, and he would be done for. Uphill travel is slow, and the animals could overtake him.

By now, the wolves had stopped gnawing at the bones. There was no meat on them, anway. Thompson heard one of the brutes beginning to howl belligerently, as if ready to attack. The other beasts howled too, now. It was an eerie, bone-chilling sound on the lonely, faraway mountain, and when Thompson later told of the adventure, he still got chills about the sound. "I thought it meant my death," Thompson told a friend some years afterward. "The awful cry carried across the valley and was echoed by the mountains."

Suddenly all six animals lined up. Were they about to rush him? They bared their sharp teeth. They lifted their snouts. Thompson's life hung by a shred. He later said he had wished he had a gun just then. He admitted that the hairs at the back of his head had stood up. A cold, clammy shiver kept going over his skin. In his Norwegian boyhood he had heard so much about famished timber wolves of the North that he felt a genuine fear. His lips went dry. His heart must have beat horribly in his chest. He perspired.

But he knew he could no longer hesitate. He had to show a bold front. He mustn't flinch in what he had to do. These wolves were like savage dogs who become even meaner when they smell a man's sweat.

With lightning speed Thompson brandished his long ski pole. He slashed it into the snow. This put his skis in motion. Thompson soared a few yards past the beasts, then glided swiftly downward.

The Norwegian didn't look back until he was at the bottom of the valley slope. The wild animals had returned to their bones. Many years later, after Dan De Quille listened to Thompson's story, the reporter put down some unforgettable words about the incident: "Snowshoe Thompson passed the wolves as a general moves along in front of his soldiers."

To go on was a cunning thing to do, and it saved Thompson's life. But when he was finally safe amid the boulders at the bottom of the valley, Thompson was still so shaken that he had to lean against a tree. "My knees almost buckled," Thompson told Postmaster Thatcher when he delivered the mail.

During his early mail trips Thompson had other narrow escapes. He realized that in all its beauty, the mountain world could be heartless, too. It shows no pity to those who venture into it. And Thompson learned that it takes as much knowledge as sheer luck to survive in it. One spring day he had stopped by the side of an especially steep hill. He was just eating a dry biscuit when he heard a monstrous roar. The air trembled. The

thundering noise paralyzed his throat. He no longer dared to swallow. Less than a mile ahead of him, the whole mountain seemed to topple. From under the summit, snow masses had broken loose and were crashing and pounding downward, picking up more snow and rocks as they cascaded. A strong wind blew into Thompson's face, and he had to plant his long pole so as not to be knocked over by the sudden air pressure. The avalanche had grown in size, rumbling and bellowing, dislodging huge boulders that were in its path, pulling out the few trees scattered across the mountain, and sending up huge clouds of snow dust.

Then all was still. A man would have been squashed to death by such a slide.

From then on, Thompson learned all he could about avalanches. He found out that entire villages in the Sierras and the Rockies had been buried, often leaving no survivors. He learned where avalanches struck. And on each trip thereafter, Thompson observed his surroundings even more keenly. He took a fresh look at steep, bare ravines and chutes. Here avalanches were likely to go after a heavy snowfall or in abruptly warming weather. Thompson talked to other people, especially those who had lived in the higher mountains longer than he. Thus he found out that rainstorms could bring down the snowy artillery. He also learned that heavily timbered slopes were safer for passage. And he figured out correctly that crests were safest of all.

This has remained a rule ever since. Nowadays few skiers would dare into the high regions alone; unless a mountain is patrolled, they go in pairs. Even so, modern skiers venturing into avalanche country trail a long, red cord behind them. The cord will indicate their position if they get swallowed by snow.

In the supervised ski areas heavy guns are actually used for shooting down slides.

Thompson had no choice but to go alone. His job demanded it. He therefore never forgot the spot where he'd seen the monster slide. The particular slope was always rooted in his mind. Indeed, during the following winters Thompson showed his courage by choosing better routes. No one doubts today that he did a smart thing.

He was a brave man, but not a foolish one. Thompson wanted to live!

VII Silver Discovery

DESPITE ALL his dangers and hardships, Snowshoe Thompson made from thirty to thirty-five round trips each winter, carrying 50 to 80 pounds on his back. No moods of nature or of man could stop him. He didn't mind either. He was used to the gales, and he quickly got used to being underpaid by the post office. He had been promised $750 for a winter's work, but every postmaster he asked referred Thompson to another postmaster. All in all, Thompson officially received only $82 for the first two winters of mail carrying. This was not enough for a livelihood. But Thompson had the respect of the miners, who would pay him a pinch of gold dust or give him a few coins for each delivered letter.

Soon he was carrying additional loads of urgently needed medicines and vital drugs such as chloroform, as he had done for Sisson. For the women he carried sewing needles and ribbon cloth, which he bought at their request in Placerville or Carson City. He brought them bonnets and yarn and even buttons, and all the while he never failed to tuck away a little free candy for the children in the faraway mining camps. When tobacco was scarce in the small settlements of prospectors, it was Thompson —the nonsmoker—who would bring it from the city stores across the snowdrifts in the mountains. He carried pots and pans, parcels and books, and groceries of all kinds on his back. People trusted this quiet Scandinavian, and they had reason to. At a time when people were often dishonest, when miners stole and lied, Thompson always made his deliveries with never an item missing. "A dependable man, that Thompson," people would say. Older folks gave him money to buy certain things in Sacramento, too, because he could get over the mountains and they could not. Thompson always returned with the merchandise he had been asked to get, and he could account for every penny he'd been given.

It seems that he failed only once. That was when Mrs. Sandy Bowers asked him to get a "peepstone" from Sacramento.

Thompson had never heard of that item.

"It's a glass ball shaped like an egg," Mrs. Bowers explained. "It should be perfectly transparent."

"What use do you make of it?"

Mrs. Bowers told Thompson that she could predict the future with a peepstone and find thieves with it and even see the faces of the dead. Next time Thompson reached Sacramento, he checked with every jewelry store, hardware store, and glassware store, determined to find the crystal ball for Mrs. Bowers. People laughed at him, and he had to laugh himself, although the lady was disappointed.

Yet Thompson never disappointed the miners in tucked-away places like Johnstown, Dogtown, and Dayton. He regularly arrived with his mailbag, rain or shine. He also made a name for himself for his great strength. Men saw him drag half a beef up a slope that slanted like the steepest ramp, and it was Thompson who was destined to move the *Territorial Enterprise,* the famous newspaper and Dan De Quille's place of work. As soon as it was decided in November, 1859, that the paper should change its first location in Genoa to its new one in Carson City, Thompson was sent for. Could he lug the heavy rolls of newsprint over the hills? Thompson did, on his skis. Well, could he also help move some of the dismantled printing presses? He did, traveling many miles. When he came back, he was asked to carry other heavy supplies. Thompson was again called for a second move when the paper decided that Virginia City, Nevada, with its thriving population, was the best site. Of course Thompson was paid for these services. He charged the rate of fifty cents a pound for commercial enterprises and for packages. He proved so reliable that even Wells, Fargo & Company asked him to take loads. FORWARD TO JOHN THOMPSON read their label.

His mail carrying was enough in demand that he could make occasional summer trips too, in addition to running his small farm near Sacramento. Industrious as he was, he also took on the job of driving stages, which meant the transport of people in addition to mail. Fortunately, a man meanwhile helped to care for Thompson's fields.

One June day Snowshoe Thompson became part of an important historical event in the mining camps. With Thompson as a link, a treasure of millions of dollars in ore was eventually found. Soon gold would no longer be king here. Silver would take its place.

It all started after two brothers—Hosea and Allen Grosh—had studied an area near Virginia City. The brothers were certain that they had stumbled onto the trail of a rich silver ore lode. But before they could find the funds to exploit their find, both men came to grief. In September, 1857, Hosea drove a miner's pick into his foot and died from the injury. His brother, Allen, in search of financial help for the mine, attempted to cross the Sierras just when Thompson was miles away and couldn't come to his rescue. Allen had never bothered to ask for directions or to get a guide; besides, he owned no skis. Allen Grosh got stranded in a blizzard. Almost dying from hunger, he devoured his mule. When he tried to drag himself through the deep snow, his matches got wet. He had no food for almost a week, and no one knew his whereabouts. By the time Allen finally hobbled back to town, he'd frozen both feet. In December, 1857, he died from gangrene, taking his silver secrets with him into the grave.

Another man, H. T. P. Comstock, who already owned many mines, was to get rich instead. After taking over the Grosh cabin, Comstock saw the prospectors at work in nearby Six-Mile Canyon. They were Peter O'Riley and Pat McLaughlin. It didn't escape Comstock that the men's rockers were heavy with blue metal. It turned out to be valuable gold and silver.

Comstock was a shrewd man and, as historians have proved, also a dishonest one. "You're on my land," Comstock told the prospectors. "I staked this claim first." O'Riley and McLaughlin didn't check on this, and Comstock talked hard. The water rights were his, too, but since they were good workers, he would take them in as "partners." The two fooled men agreed to this.

But just how valuable was the silver ore? It had to be assayed, but who could be trusted to take a sample for analysis in California?

O'Riley knew Thompson, and that June day—while the three prospectors stayed behind to continue working—Thompson was asked to rush the sample for assaying. Would the carrier please hurry back with the assaying result? Thompson promised to do his best.

He wrapped the ore sample into a piece of checkered shirt. Then he walked at a fast clip to Virginia City. Here he saddled a horse and galloped as speedily as he could to Carson City. The route from there, though bumpy, was flat enough, and Thompson could make excellent time until the road began to curve and rise before Woodfords. From there on to Strawberry Station it was tough riding. The spring thaws had caused a lot of water to flood the thoroughfare, rutting it and making it full of holes. The ore sample tucked away safely in his pocket, Thompson trotted past hundreds of wagons that had got stuck and been left abandoned on the highway by their owners. Thompson's horse stumbled across wagon wheels that lay buried in the mud. His horse's hooves struck wooden boxes, pieces of furniture, and even old pianos that had been dumped to lighten the vehicles. Shortly, Thompson crossed what is now Echo Summit, and then he descended to follow along the American River.

Thompson reached Placerville in a couple of days. He naturally wondered why he shouldn't use the services of an assayer right there where he knew many people. But he had his orders. He was to ride to Grass Valley, northeast of Sacramento, California. So he struck out northwest in the direction of what is today the location of Auburn, and from there, he headed north along a dusty road to the town called Grass Valley. It seemed that Grass Valley had excellent assayers. But knowing as much

as he did about mining, Thompson must have guessed still another reason for the long journey: the farther away an assay was made, the better a secret could be kept from the people in Comstock's own territory.

Comstock and his companions wanted certainty about the blue ore. So they'd asked Thompson to get in touch with Judge James Walsh as soon as he arrived in Grass Valley. The judge was known for his mining knowledge, and he would know the best assayers in town. Walsh turned out to be a shrewd, cautious man. He thought that it would be best to use two assayers, working independently.

It was already evening when Thompson and the judge finally got to Melville Atwood's office, which had closed by now. They summoned the assayer at home, who was willing, despite the late hour, to run a check on the mineral find. He split the rock in half, and while he made his own analysis, working with his scales and chemicals, Thompson and his contact hurried to the second assayer, J. J. Ott, who also had his office in Grass Valley.

By midnight the two appraisals came in. The blue rock contained not only gold but indeed a fabulous amount of silver as well! The silver alone weighed out at $4,000 a ton; altogether the Ophir Mine would yield $13,000,000 worth of metals. Other Comstock mines also did fabulously well.

Back in Nevada, O'Riley, McLaughlin, and Comstock had made only one mistake. They had tapped Judge Walsh, a man who knew a treasure when he saw one. Before dawn the next day he and a friend were already traveling across the Sierras in order to buy an interest in the mine. Unfortunately Walsh and his companion also told other people in California that the Nevada diggings would be unbelievably rich, and soon the news

—which Thompson had tried to keep secret—began to spread as far away as the West Coast. Thousands of miners flocked across the mountains before winter. Farmers left their Oregon land. In San Francisco clerks deserted their offices. Loggers, ironworkers, gardeners, butlers, and dishwashers turned into Washoe miners. Silver! Their mad zeal must have reminded John Thompson of the discovery at John Sutter's mill ten years earlier. The color had been gold then, and it brought droves of people to California. They were called the forty-niners because they arrived in 1849; the new armies of silver prospectors were the fifty-niners, although they still came later.

Practically overnight, Thompson witnessed how new towns rose where not a stick had stood before. Gold Hill, a mile from the Ophir Mine, grew. Silver City was born. Gold Camp sprouted. Virginia City became a jumble of canvas tents, rickety shanties, tents made of potato sacks, tin huts, miserable earth hovels, blankets stretched across poles to house men, and little one-person caves called dugouts, burrowed out of the mountains. Rough barracks were nailed together to lodge miners at a dollar a bed. Few permanent dwellings stood in Six-Mile Canyon, where Thompson had been engaged as the ore courier.

Thompson couldn't believe his eyes at what he had helped to bring about! Thousands of wagons now creaked and squished across his beloved mountains. The silver-seekers came by mule, donkey, and horse, sometimes with their women and children. Those who owned no pack animals struggled across the furrowed mud mountains on foot, the men themselves loaded like burros. Once more Thompson saw prospectors pushing their wheelbarrows loaded with mining picks, dynamite, shovels, blankets, bedrolls, pans for silver panning, and pans for frying.

Wealthy gentlemen in top hats and dark suits arrived from San Francisco in shaking, bouncing private stages. Quickly recovering from the journey, they rushed to buy red flannel shirts, rugged pants, and high boots, and thus went to stake their mining claims. Families who had taken their oxen and farm wagons to the West Coast in search of gold there now came to John Thompson's country to seek silver. They were followed by the big promoters and by those who sold mining supplies. Teamsters drove overloaded wagons pulled by as many as ten horses at one time.

That fall, and for several years after, the whole Washoe district (named after the Washoe Mountains) was havoc. Thompson found old Norwegian friends from his days in the Midwest, but he also saw Swedes, Finns, Germans, Swiss, Scandinavians, Irishmen, Scotsmen, South Americans, Chinese. Arriving from abroad, they often couldn't understand each other. English was the common language, naturally, but some of the people knew only their native tongue. *"Mucha plata!"* (Much silver) cried Mexican miners. *"Viel Silber!"* shouted some Austrian youths who'd come west searching for fortunes. In their thirst for treasure, which Thompson never shared, men often acted like rascals. Cheating was commonplace.

Indeed, Thompson's home grounds were settled by some strange types. Men posed as preachers and collected money. Some fellows claimed that they were doctors and practiced medicine without a license or with a fake one. Thousands of miners thus died from the rough living conditions. The phony doctors just couldn't help them, and real physicians were scarce. Other men died from the bad water or from illnesses easily cured today.

At the Ophir and other Comstock mines—in time, there would be twenty of these—workmen were employed to labor underground, too. Many people came to grief when tunnels collapsed. Often workers would get their heads blown off from exploding dynamite. And deep down, their arms or legs would be chopped by falling boulders. One poor fellow even got his head sliced away at the neck by a mining cage that descended too fast. In all the excitement, tempers flared. Men would fight over nothing more than a silver nugget. They would get so angry at lawyers' offices that they'd discharge their pistols at one another.

Even schoolteachers wore revolvers. The worst fights broke out at night because the men were drinking. Sometimes dozens of miners would then hit each other over the head with bottles or fists. There was no sheriff yet to separate them and to seek out the guilty ones. Miners took care of their own rough justice. While they battled—or slept—Indians would steal their horses or donkeys. Masked bandits roamed Carson Valley. If someone caught a horse thief, a group of miners would get together and simply hang the man.

Fights had always left John Thompson cold. In the middle of the excitement he went his own way. He didn't like meddling in other people's business. Besides, he had his own work to do.

The winter of 1859 was an especially severe one. The winds blew, and so much snow fell that even Virginia City and Gold Hill—only two miles apart—were blocked off from each other. It was impossible, without skis, to get from Gold Hill to Silver City, only a mile away. The short distance between Woodfords and Markleeville seemed as far as a continent. Food became scarce, and grocers who had hoarded enough of it made great profits. A pound of flour, worth only a few cents, was sold for eight dollars.

A new postmaster decided that he would try a stagecoach line for transportation of mail, but of course the horses got stuck in 30-foot drifts. So the winter stagecoach idea had to be abandoned. Again Thompson took over with his snowshoes. He was a welcome sight at the marooned post offices and in the drafty tents of the miners. "Snowshoe Thompson!" the men shouted when he skied up to their makeshift quarters. "Snowshoe Thompson is coming!" children called from the dugouts.

People eagerly read their mail, hoped for more of the same, played cards, worked, quarreled, and waited desperately for spring.

It finally came. The bitter cold gave way to a blazing battle where much hot blood was to be spilled.

For the first time in his life, even the peaceful Norwegian would get involved in combat!

VIII Indian War

EARLY IN 1860 a new event threatened to change Thompson's career. That April, the first Pony Express rider sped into Carson Valley with a load of mail from St. Joseph, Missouri. Would Thompson's job now be finished? Some people thought so, for the Pony Express soon employed more than 100 relay riders and 500 horses between St. Joseph and Sacramento, a distance of almost 2,000 miles. About every tenth day a mounted carrier in buckskin, armed with a Colt six-shooter, would pound into Carson City. From here, the next rider galloped off toward California with his black leather pouch. Speedy, speedy mail. What a fantastic idea! But it lasted only eighteen months and then lost great sums of money. Horseback delivery proved too expensive, and in any case the winters were too severe. Thus, Snowshoe Thompson still kept his job.

But he wanted to be closer to the area where he and his skis were in demand in winter. He still had his cabin and a little land in Sacramento Valley, California. This was inconveniently far from Virginia City, Genoa, Dayton, and the other towns on his routes. So he now settled in the lovely Diamond Valley, some

30 miles south of Carson City. He bought a little ground; here he would grow wild hay, alfalfa, and wheat.

When the snow started thawing that spring, he went out with his tools and built first a well and then a dugout. This was just a square hole in the ground, topped by sod walls and a roof. It would have to do until Thompson could find time and money to put up a cabin. He knew that his farm could produce enough crops only if there was enough water. Thompson decided to tap a little brook which ran through his property; the brook could be connected with irrigation ditches. But this required more than one pick and shovel, as well as more pairs of hands. Especially now. There just wasn't much time if Thompson wanted to plant and harvest this year. To get on fast with the water system, Thompson therefore hired two friendly Washo Indians. The natives were as dark-haired as Thompson was blond, but they all worked quietly side by side until the task had been completed. These Indians belonged to a peaceful tribe.

Nevertheless, the 1860's were full of Indian strife. Snowshoe Thompson must surely have known about the hostile Apaches of the Southwest, or about the Cheyennes, Sioux, and Comanches in other parts of the country. After all, he liked to read the newspapers of his day, and the many uprisings and fights filled the pages of the *Territorial Enterprise*. Still, Thompson never had any personal trouble with Indians. In fact, he had a lot of sympathy for them.

Much of the Indian country had been taken over by white men. For decades the white settlers had cheated the redskins out of land and had made treaties only to break them. White men had shot the game on which the natives depended, and now there were few elk, deer, and antelope left; the Indians even had trouble finding rabbits. The days of buffalo hunting would soon be over, and that too, meant a great loss to the natives. Some tribes used field mice for food; others dug trenches to catch grasshoppers. The Indians also looked for piñon nuts. But these were getting scarce, too, because the settlers were burning the pine trees as firewood. Thompson knew that some Indians survived only on roots, weeds, and sunflowers. Or they ate what they could beg from the whites.

So it was little wonder that again and again the Indians became angry. Hostility flared often, and for some time Indian bands on both sides of the Sierras had raided farms for horses, held up stagecoaches, and stole whatever they could. Now they also attacked Pony Express personnel. They robbed wagon trains. They even rode away with captured white women.

Finally, on May 6, 1860, it happened.

To Thompson's displeasure, some whites got everyone into great trouble at Williams Station, a trading post on the Carson River. James Williams and a few others jailed three women of the Paiute tribe. It was never clear what these Indian squaws had done, if anything. In any case, two of the Paiute women were married. And that night, one of the Indian husbands, wearing soft moccasins, tiptoed to the cellar where his wife was held.

He called down through a slit of a window. His wife called back to him, tears choking her throat. At that moment, one of the guards saw the visitor. Two more whites rushed up to beat the Paiute before he could stretch his bow. James Williams, the Williams Station trader who had gotten rich by selling merchandise to the Indians, showed up, too. The white men hit and kicked the poor redskin. "Git away!" they told him. "Show your face again, and we'll shoot you full o' lead!"

The next day, some Paiute and many Bannock and Shoshoni came to free the squaws and to burn down Williams Station. The Indians then killed all the men in this trading post, including James Williams. On the way back to their camps the angry raiders slew three parties of unarmed prospectors.

Thompson was in Virginia City for supplies when even worse news reached him. A rider arriving from Pyramid Lake had seen large groups of Indians holding a war council. This meant that the Indians would soon be on the warpath. If so, they would probably attack the mining towns. Counting the Bannock, Shoshoni, and other tribes in the vicinity, such as the Pit River Indians, the Paiutes might be able to muster at least 5,000 warriors to join the fight. And just then there happened to be no regular U.S. troops in this mining country. The miners and townspeople would therefore have to man their own defenses.

At first the Carson Valley population was not sure what they should do. Would the massing Indians definitely strike at their towns? Thompson asked some other local citizens about this, and the answer left little doubt: A war couldn't be far away. Although Thompson was still unmarried, he must have thought of the women in Carson City and Virginia City. He must have considered the many children who might be hurt in the battle. Thompson was among the first to help families into the safety of barricaded stone houses. And he assisted in the hasty labor to put up forts and stockades where other women and children would be safe.

The evening of May 8 was a frantic one. All the mines had shut down, and Thompson mingled with the miners who walked around the muddy streets to talk over the threat. In every town scores of nervous men swore revenge on the Indians and said they'd fight them tooth and nail. That night many prospectors slept with their boots on, weapons at the ready.

By dawn the Indian assault hadn't come. A high pitch of excitement had gripped the region. Were the Indians preparing themselves? Or had they changed their minds? Old-timers knew that red men could turn into savages—fearless, cunning, brutal. If those Indians were well armed, they could outshoot the miners, and Indian horsemanship could be superior too. Word spread in several Carson Valley towns: An army had to be recruited. Volunteers must be fashioned into military units. Thousands promised to join. But when the sun rose, the majority of the white men just backed out. The promises were just empty words.

Then it was morning, and the Indians still had not arrived. Two white leaders came forward to take control of the situation. One was Major William M. Ormsby, who had laid out and named Carson City. Ormsby had recently become a storekeeper, and he also owned stage lines. The other leader lived in Virginia City, where he ran a law office. His name was Captain Henry Meredith. Ormsby and Meredith figured that white units had to track down the Indians before they could do more damage. The appeal to the people brought only 105 volunteers, who gathered in Virginia City.

No one is sure why Thompson joined Ormsby's small expedition. Thompson kept no journal, and he never told anyone his reasons for volunteering. Certainly he had always been a peaceful man and a stranger to hatred. Because he read the Bible so often and didn't smoke or drink, the prospectors still called him Holy John. It was also true that the Norwegian hadn't worn a gun since his first mail trips on skis, and he had always managed to avoid the badmen and the brawls. People later debated about Thompson riding to battle. Was it because he'd made a promise to Ormsby and he always kept his promises? Was it because he became aroused by the massacre at Williams Station? Or because he felt a sense of duty toward the country where he had taken roots and which valued him? All these motives were sound. But there may have been just one more, which made sense, too. Thompson wanted to protect the women and children. He undoubtedly knew many families in the imperiled towns.

Soon Ormsby's volunteers rode out of Virginia City. They skirted what is now Reno, Nevada, and then headed east toward Pyramid Lake. Thompson had hung the revolver onto his belt, and his companions had shouldered muskets and shotguns. None of the men wore uniforms; they'd come to fight in their baggy, padded pants. They wore slouchy hats, and they had dirty bedrolls strapped to their saddles. It was a three-day ride, and at night they made camp in a forest, where they cooked their beans. In the morning, Ormsby gave the signal to ride on, and the bearded, tobacco-chewing would-be army gave their horses the spurs. "We'll slaughter those Indians! Every last one of them!" they told Thompson. He listened to the boasts and kept silent. He knew that some men—especially the new arrivals from the East who didn't know Indian warfare—had come because they thirsted for adventure. According to historians, Ormsby's strange army was further composed of hay farmers, stagemen, gamblers, and tavernkeepers who wanted the Indians' horses. And some other Carson Valley citizens thought that it was just a lark. Several rowdies gulped down whiskey all the way to Williams Station.

The outpost had indeed been burned to the ground. Of what

had been a store, just a few blackened metal containers and a potbellied stove remained. The bodies of the felled white men still lay there. But the Indians were gone. Would they still be at their headquarters near Pyramid Lake?

Pyramid Lake is 35 miles long and partly encircled by craggy rock formations and sheer cliffs. It took until May 12 to come within sight of the lake. The men halted and held their breaths. All was still. Thompson had expected tepees or other Indian abodes, but there were none. Ormsby gave orders to push on. The major rode ahead. The narrowing route led along the Truckee River. To Thompson's right the hill rose steeply, and all at once he saw mounted Indians on top of the rocks. Their faces were painted white, contrasting with their long black hair.

Thompson heard their war whoops. At the same time the first arrows started swishing downward. Other Indian braves were armed with shotguns. They aimed well from the mountaintop. Ormsby's column returned the fire, but the ambush had come so suddenly that a few miners were already dead. Then the Indians did a strange thing. When Ormsby's surprised units started to shoot, the Paiutes, Bannocks, and Shoshonis fled across the hilltops. Once in a while they stopped to pull triggers. Then they were out of sight.

"Follow them!" Major Ormsby commanded. The white men, with Thompson among them, rode in pursuit through the valley. The horses were just ready to climb the ravine when all at once 300 new Indians blocked the road. Three hundred against one hundred! The poisoned arrows and the rifle bullets whistled and smacked into the surprised whites. Ormsby wheeled his horse; the Indians who had fled to lure the troops deeper into

the canyon now materialized at the other end, right behind them. It had been a crafty trick.

John Thompson and his companions were in a trap.

Being encircled and outnumbered made for a bad situation. Worse still, the horses of Ormsby's volunteers were tired from the long journey, whereas the Indians rode fresh animals. Few settlers had any experience in fighting the clever natives, who were led brilliantly by the son of Chief Winnemucca, a Bannock. It was to be an uneven battle, and Winnemucca swiftly had the upper hand over Ormsby. The Indian volleys found their mark while the confused whites proved bad shots.

Thompson's own revolver was soon empty, and he had never been much good at this, anyway. Near him, Captain Meredith was one of the first to be wounded. An Indian bullet hit him with such impact that Meredith tumbled from his horse. A courageous man, he kept discharging his pistol from the ground, but then a fatal shot got him. Confusion reigned now.

"Regroup in the woods!" Major Ormsby shouted.

The citizens swiveled their ponies toward the cottonwood trees, blasting away as they went. But the Indians, still hurling war whoops into the smoky air, sped into the forest, too. Some of the warriors were as young as fourteen, and they showed no fear at all. To their elders, fighting like this was a pleasure.

Unfortunately, Ormsby's army didn't manage to regroup. The major then ordered his troops to make a stand. But more men fell. Again and again, the Indians were superior in hand-to-hand combat. Bowie knives and rifle barrels struck incessantly. Before the sun went down, Thompson saw Major Ormsby being whacked down by an Indian tomahawk. Bleeding from both arms, the major fought on from behind a tree. Finally, a Paiute bullet wounded him mortally.

With both commanders dead, total disorder had come to the whites. It was each citizen for himself now, battling as best he could. Some miners who still controlled their horses dismounted. Using their animals as shields, several men fought until all their ammunition was gone. Thompson saw how arrows kept riddling the beasts, and he figured, correctly, that more than half the expedition was already wiped out. In the noise of the battle, many of the horses ran away, to be caught by the Indians.

The survivors had no choice but to retreat. However, with the Indians at their heels, this was difficult, too. Most whites were in panic. From the ground, fallen men moaned terribly. But according to eyewitnesses, Thompson still remained cool. Perhaps it was his Scandinavian blood. He realized that *someone* had to call for help, and he hoped to be the one. He quickly surveyed the bloody scene; the Indian corral was still around him. Or was there an opening? Thompson discovered that only a handful of braves guarded the Truckee River. He rode straight toward them, reached the shore, let his horse jump into the water, and made it swim across. All the while, the surprised Indians shot after him, but missing.

To Thompson's astonishment, a battle also raged across the river. Several of Ormsby's men had managed to get there before Thompson.

But they were again outnumbered by Indians.

To make better time, the fleeing volunteers threw away blankets and bedrolls and pans and other gear. Many lost their weapons, too.

The war tables had turned. First the palefaces pursued the redskins through the canyon into a death trap. Now the Indians rode after the routed whites. Indeed, the Bannocks and Paiutes hunted their prey with a murder-mad fury.

There seemed to be no escape. Thompson had not covered more than a mile when his horse was shot out from under him. The mail carrier jumped to his long feet and ran behind the next boulder. Below him a mountain curved downward, and Thompson later told Dan De Quille, the reporter: "I desperately wished the whole valley were buried in snow and I were on my skis." In a downhill trip on snow, he would have outraced any Indian arrow.

Instead, Thompson was on foot now and dashing from one boulder to the next for cover. Dead bodies were all around. Thompson kept running. Suddenly a man next to him shouted that there was a loose horse. "It's following you! Look!" Thompson spun about, and there was a horse all right. All saddled and bridled and without a master. In an interview with De Quille, Thompson later said, "I believe that the Lord sent that horse." If it hadn't been there, Thompson would surely have been slain.

As it was, he flung himself into the saddle and managed to get away. He had cause to, for the Indians showed no mercy now. They kept after the whites for 20 miles, killing every miner they could find. That night white prisoners were scalped while Indians danced around them. Of the 105 men who had started out with great confidence, 76 were killed. A dozen more were wounded. The Indians lost only three.

The rest of the story is well preserved by history. When Thompson and the trickle of survivors arrived with the news of defeat in Virginia City, the mining towns were thrown into panic. Masses of people took off for California. Others fled to Utah. In fear of the victors, men built more stockades. Other defenders hollowed out trees and stuffed them with gunpowder in the hope of firing these crude cannons. Men hid in deep mine shafts. One farmer was so scared of the Indians that he had someone lower him into the bottom of a dry well. The helper ran out of town to save his own skin, and it was three days before the fellow was found in the well, more dead than alive.

Thompson saw only one way out. Regular U.S. Army troops from California had to come. The Paiutes, Shoshonis, and Bannocks had to be subdued, or there would never be peace. So Thompson rode to Sacramento, from where he'd once fetched chloroform for the miner named Sisson. This time Thompson helped to bring the troop reinforcements that would make an end to the redskin danger, at least in this region. The blue-coated American soldiers came from Sacramento with howitzer cannons, and heavily armed infantrymen rode out of Downieville, California. These troops were joined by volunteers, and on June 2, 1860, the Indians were finally vanquished. The victory took place at Pyramid Lake, near the spot where the Indians had made their big ambush.

Fortunately, the white men soon changed their tactics in Carson Valley. Instead of war, they made peace. Someone, for instance, found the funds to build a sawmill for the Paiutes. Indians were encouraged to earn money in the towns' forges and shops and mines or to help the ranchers for pay. Indian agents gave the braves farming tools, horses, blankets, and other gifts. They presented the women with needles, thread, and calico cloth. This was a good idea, for kindness usually reaps rewards. One day an old Paiute arrived too late for the distribution of shirts. The Indian affairs agent took off his own shirt and handed it to the Paiute.

This way, Snowshoe Thompson's country had at last become quiet.

Thompson could go back to his own work.

IX Man Against Snow

AGAIN THE SNOW came down from the Sierra skies like a million feathers. Snow covered the sand around Lake Tahoe and fell onto the black surface of the water, melting. Snow heaped on the large pine cones and on the bleached fallen tree branches at the foot of Genoa Peak. Monument Peak had its head in the snow clouds, and snow piled up on the passes, on the black mining machinery in the cities, and in the miner's sluice boxes. The sagebrush and evergreens of Carson Valley were pushed down by the white masses, and all the trails and roads disappeared in the drifts.

Snows accumulated in the high Sierras, where work on a railroad came to a standstill. It was to be a severe winter.

The white mantle spread over Diamond Valley; here Thompson's farm had increased in size. Thanks to the Homestead Act, he now had 160 acres for the asking; these yielded bigger crops. His fruit trees, though leafless now in winter, were going to do well. Smoked hams hung in the larder. His abode had grown. The dugout served as cellar for his new log cabin. One room even had a fireplace.

Not that he had the chance like other folks to sit by the fireside during the winters. He was much too busy for that. At the post offices they once more waited and hoped for Snowshoe Thompson. Placerville and Genoa and Woodfords and Murphy's Camp and many other communities still counted on him. With snows piling up to a depth of 50 feet, there were not only letters but packages, medicines, candy, household goods and verbal messages by people who couldn't write. Miners also called on Thompson to climb the hills with quarters of beef on his strong back. After all, he had a better stance on his skis than any man on boots. The *Enterprise*, where Mark Twain had made a name for himself, asked Thompson to carry bundles of newspapers that described the Civil War. He skied up and down the old Emigrant Road in search of the lost and to pull out sleighs that had become stuck. Now in his tenth year on the job, he still hadn't got lost himself. "Something here in my head keeps me right," he'd answer when people asked him how he did it. But those who knew Thompson best claimed that he had an uncanny sense of direction and that, as the years went by, he knew the landmarks on his wintry route better than anyone else. There were few men who could have matched him on these cold treks; only Thompson had the strength and patience and self-reliance for the mileage.

He needed it all, too. Once, in a rush to get his postal bag, he forgot his food. He went on for the full three days it took to Placerville without a speck of nourishment, then made up for it. A few weeks later he bent over a frozen river for a drink. Promptly the little metal box in which he now carried his matches fell into the water. He stuck his hand into the icy slit.

Too late. That night he'd have to get along without a fire. As the chilly air began to penetrate him, he tried an old Norwegian folk dance which he remembered from childhood. The wild hops kept him alive until dawn finally came. He would have to endure another Sierra blizzard the next evening. The wind drove snow against his face like so many pins, but he went on. If he'd stopped, he would have perished. His continuing that night was all the more remarkable because he traveled alone. Unlike Arctic explorers who have gone through similar ordeals, Thompson had no dogs for company. He had no other men who could rescue him. He was always forced to be his own rescuer.

One bad day the winter fury found him in Hermit Valley, which is as good a name as any. The gale made him search out a deserted mountain cabin. In those days there was nothing unusual about a man's taking over another's house during a nasty night; the visitor was expected only to leave someone else's belongings alone and to clean up in the morning. But that particular evening it had snowed so much that only the cabin's chimney stuck out. Thompson had foreseen this and brought some firewood from the valley. Now he undid the bundle and tossed stick after stick through the chimney. The wood would keep him warm in the house. And tonight warmth was everything. After the last piece had plopped through the opening, Thompson let the mailbag down on a string. Then he himself stepped into the chimney. At first it was wide enough for his broad shoulders; in fact, he could even keep his feet braced against the rough walls. But when he crawled farther down, the chimney narrowed. He hadn't figured on that. He took a deep breath and pulled in his chest. He went down a little way. But suddenly Thompson could go no farther. He was wedged in the chimney, long feet dangling. The rough walls pressed into his arms and hips, and for an instant he just hung there. He tried to muster his muscle power and then to edge upward. It didn't work. He was imprisoned.

Snowshoe Thompson was stuck like this for more than an hour. Then he summoned all his remaining strength until he could wiggle and inch and push his way down to safety. That night, after making a fire, Thompson slept a little. In the morning he faced another harrowing chore. He had to find a way to pry open the snow-choked front door and then dig himself out of the winter-buried house. This took many hours. When he at last skied away, he was bruised and scraped and tired.

But every winter he skied more powerfully. He seldom took more than fifteen hours for the 90 up-and-down miles between Placerville and Genoa. Reporter Dan De Quille wrote at the time, "Thompson, with a heavy bag upon his back, has frequently run three miles in five minutes. He has command of his shoes to such an extent that he glides among the obstructions like a skater on ice; at ever so great a speed he will touch or pass within an inch of any designated object."

Thompson would also lace his trips with ski jumps; he easily leaped 50 to 60 feet and didn't come to grief. An account by W. P. Merrill, then postmaster of Woodfords, tells us that Thompson even "made a jump of one-hundred and eighty feet without a break." When Dan De Quille learned of this record, he just couldn't believe it. He considered the postmaster a reliable man, though, and to be absolutely certain, De Quille talked to other sources, too. Yes, they said. It was the truth. Thompson had made these giant leaps, sure enough.

The word spread in Carson Valley, and on many hills boys

were suddenly trying to jump off the knolls. All over the Sierra foothills men would imitate Thompson; they would steer their long, upcurved skis toward a sharp dropoff, flex their leg muscles and then—still standing straight up—hurl themselves into the air. This way, they'd fly above the snowy ground as far as they could and then land again. But Thompson had created a fashion in other ways, too. In numerous mining camps men were building skis, which some people still called snowshoes. And in many parts of Nevada and California folks were experimenting with these runners. The enthusiasm knew no bounds. One man even outfitted his horse with short skis that went under the hooves.

Thompson was not alone in spreading the gospel. Other Scandinavians had meanwhile arrived in the region to show their skills, too. *Skis!* Skis made everything possible. They kept miners healthy who had to spend many hours underground and desperately needed fresh air. The exercise also put a glow on the cheeks of farm youngsters and warmed the limbs of office workers. But more important, these long slices of spruce or oak began to serve as winter transportation. Youths in the mining camps could now visit one another. Children were able to reach snow-marooned schoolhouses. Some midwives arrived on wooden boards to deliver babies, and doctors visited the sick this way. Women in long skirts slid to church, and even preachers paid visits on skis. Life in the forlorn camps was no longer lonely.

Of course Snowshoe Thompson—the most experienced skier of all—was asked to teach what he knew best. He freely gave his time to small children and big children and adults.

In 1866 one of his pupils included a soft-spoken, sweetly

smiling girl named Agnes Singleton. A few years earlier Agnes had come to Genoa from Preston, England, chaperoned by her mother. Thompson got to know Agnes through an uncle of hers who owned a nearby ranch. The Singletons immediately liked the Norwegian. He at once made an impression on the English girl, too. And why not? His lean figure, his piercing blue eyes, and his well-kept blond beard in a weather-beaten face were all a striking sight. As for Thompson, he was intrigued by Agnes' English accent, and he often spoke to others about her cheerfulness. All that winter Thompson visited her, and soon he was coaching Agnes on the white slopes, too. Naturally, one day, he could stop himself no longer. He asked Agnes Singleton to be his bride.

They were married in a small church at Empire, near Carson City. A year later, on February 11, 1867, they had a son, whom they named Arthur. They made a fine family, and marriage was good for Thompson.

He no longer had to bake his own bread or flip his own flapjacks. The slight copper-haired girl did it all for him. She cooked, she washed, she cleaned, she helped in the fields. Friends later also remembered that the English girl excelled in growing berries, which she harvested and canned. Elderberries. Gooseberries. Service berries. Rose berries. Currants. Roundfaced Arthur must have been as delighted with the fruit pies as his father was. On his end, Thompson built all the furniture, which included the tables, chairs, stools, benches, and even a bed. He bought a cooking stove and many new pots and pans for Agnes; he even made the house still bigger by adding several rooms.

But now that Snowshoe Thompson had a wife and child, he began to be more worried about money. The post office had made a lot of promises, but it paid Thompson for only two winters. Here and there he collected a little something from the people to whom he delivered letters and for the freight. There was enough to eat, but at thirty-nine, Thompson was still a poor man.

One day, he saw a poster: SNOWSHOE RACE. The winner would get a six-hundred-dollar purse.

"You ought to try it," Agnes said. "You're the best skier in the world!"

Thompson didn't say anything, but perhaps his wife was right. Perhaps he should enter the meet. It was possible that he could outrace others. A friend had once clocked him between Meadowlake and Cisco. It was a four-mile downhill stretch, and he had completed it in four minutes. So he'd done 60 miles an hour! Yet he'd never tried to enter a contest, although these races often made news. There is evidence that miners competed on snowshoes as far back as the mid-1850's in Onion Valley, California. Thompson surely must have learned about the prospectors who competed at Johnsville, Sawpit Flat, and Grassflat to see who was the fastest.

The six-hundred-dollar event was sponsored by the Alturas Ski Club of La Porte, California. This was some 200 miles away from Diamond Valley, and one winter day Thompson packed a little dried venison, some biscuits, and his matches, said goodbye to his wife, and took off across the mountains.

La Porte was not easy to get to. First of all, Thompson had to surmount a wooded mountain pass. He took a ferry across Lake Tahoe, put his skis back on near the present-day Incline

Village, and then plotted his course across the hills to Truckee. Here he boarded a train to Colfax, then traveled by stage via Nevada City to Comptonville, from where he trudged another full night with a lantern until he reached La Porte and the meet.

When Thompson told the people from where he'd come, he reaped a lot of admiration. Why, what a journey! And of course they'd heard of him and were glad that he could spare a long weekend. Some of the racers had already assembled. Old photos show how these men looked: they wore the same rough work pants which served them in the mines. The pants were often held up by suspenders, and a few men put on white shirts for the race occasion. High boots were the rule, too. As for the skis, they pretty much matched Snowshoe Thompson's. Depending on a fellow's size, his boards were from 9 to 12 feet long, 4 to 8½ inches wide, and 1¼ inches thick in the center. Charles Hendel, a mining engineer of those long-gone days, reported that the "snow-shoes [skis] are tapered at the top from near the middle to ¼ of an inch in thickness at the toes, and nearly flat. The toes are turned up like sleigh runners. They are nearly of uniform width from end to end—a little wider, if any, on the front—and a spring is worked in, so that without weights they rest on the heels and points; but when the rider stands on them, the weight is somewhat evenly distributed, and a concave groove is made at the bottom, beginning near the toes and running to the heels, similar to the bottom of the skates."

The racecourse suited Thompson fine. It was very steep, leading past tree stumps and boulders and straight down over half-buried bushes. Thompson was used to bigger mountains, of course; this one provided only about 1,400 feet of running. At the bottom was the "finish gate," consisting of wooden posts with flags. Men with stop watches would stand there during the meet. The mountaintop was reached on foot, with the miners shouldering their long planks. By 10 A.M. everybody, including Thompson, had to be up on top. There were about thirty racers. Some had come from towns with strange names like Whiskey Diggings and Port Wine, but many also lived in Plumas County and La Porte.

Excited spectators already lined the racecourse, which was marked by more wooden posts. Tension hung in the air. Bets were being made. Which of the represented towns would have the best racers? Would anyone break his leg? Who had invented a new magic lubricant for swifter snowshoes?

But there was still some delay. The racers had work to do. The skis had to run well. When Snowshoe talked to some of the miners, he was told that he had to do more than just sandpaper and polish the undersides of his skis. No, you could only get real speeds with special mixtures. The men called it dope, and Thompson noticed several people who had no other job but to mix the high-speed formulas. Racing had become "scientific," they claimed. The mailman was puzzled. Some dope makers were painting the ski bottom with something that smelled like pine tar; others were brushing turpentine, cedar oils, beeswax, candle wax, and even shoe polish onto their gear. A few competitors were already skating around on their skis to try out the dope men's products. Shoe polish for his mail route? Well, maybe yes. The mixtures made sense in spring when the snow would stick to everyone's boards. Thompson had to agree; he had often encountered that problem, which was one reason for his night travel in the mountains. But the time was winter now and not spring, so Thompson just kept watching the dope men.

One ancient type had placed a kettle over the fire. Thompson asked him about the steaming, bubbling, many-colored liquid.

"A secret," the man answered.

Thompson inquired again.

"Well, just call it 'Sierra lightning.' "

Snowshoe Thompson had never used anything like it, and because he was a newcomer to the La Porte races, a dope maker was willing to lend a hand. Would Thompson like some glassy-looking stuff to speed up his downhill run? But the mail carrier shook his head. Perhaps he felt that he would go fast anyway.

All the time, more people were arriving on horse-drawn sleighs and on snowshoes from nearby towns; even the local priests, barbers and saloonkeepers had taken the day off, and certainly there were large crowds of women and children, all ready to watch. Soon the miners were grouped into fours, usually one from each town.

There would be an elimination race; the competitors who fell once would get another chance, and all the winners would ski against one another until there was only the best man left. He'd get the purse. A starter gave the signal by shooting a gun, and the first four were off, with wild yells and cheers from the onlookers.

Thompson could see right away that they had a style different from his own. He stood up on skis; these fellows squatted down. They had one long staff like his, but they kept it between their legs for braking, which he'd never done. Sometimes men would crash, and other contestants would pile into them. On other occasions before Thompson's own start, a miner would strike a competitor's skis on purpose to make him careen off course. Several men smashed into trees. It was a rough game, and it didn't suit the well-mannered Norwegian. But the run was short, and it all ended in less than a minute. The first man to reach bottom was the winner who would have to battle it out with other winners.

"John Thompson!"

Thompson went to the start, and people pointed to him because he was so well known. The other three men turned out to be Isaac Frank Steward of La Porte, James Gould of Gibsonville, and C. Scott of Poker Flat. Steward was the best-known among the trio; the townspeople called him "world champion."

The four men now took their positions side by side, like track runners.

The Scandinavian eyed them as they were ready to stab their poles into the snow before pushing off. Should he go down on his haunches too? Would it really be faster? But when the gun signal burst into the sky, his years of habit got the better of him. He stood up. He went very fast, but the others were faster. In the second heat he did no better. A little disappointed, he traveled the 200 miles home. There he let it be known through the newspaper that he invited the people who'd beaten him to try again. He suggested a race "from the top to the bottom of the highest, heaviest-timbered mountain, with a precipice fifteen feet high, the one jumping without falling being the winner."

Shortly Thompson got his answer from the Alturas Ski Club. "We won't make business for doctors and undertakers," they wrote back. The races continued on the short stretches of Lexington Hill in La Porte, on Eureka Peak, near Johnsville in Jamison City, and at a place called Howland Flat. All sorts of speed records were established, with one man even timed at 87 miles per hour.

But Snowshoe Thompson's challenge of longer runs and jumps was never taken up. Thompson had his day all the same. A few years later he invited the region's best snowshoers to beat him down Silver Mountain, California. There were 200 competitors. The course was not charted, and Thompson came in first.

As often in his life, he'd forgotten all about the money. And it turned out that this time the miners had raced just for the fun of it.

There was no purse.

But a few years later there was a large sum on the horizon. In fact, it would be the biggest stake Thompson had ever faced.

X Faster Than the Iron Horse

SUDDENLY THINGS moved swiftly for Thompson.

Some Nevada state officials had long heard about Thompson's heroic, underpaid labors. The time had come to reward the mail carrier for his years of service. The Nevada legislature sprang into action. It was decided that Thompson should get $6,000 in back wages.

A petition was drawn up. It was signed by Governor James W. Nye in Carson City. It was signed by other state officials and by all the local postmasters. Then the paper passed on to the people in Carson Valley. Man after man put down his name in favor of Snowshoe Thompson. The governor's office next took the petition to the other side of the Sierras. Here, too, the signatures lined the document.

About 1,000 people had signed.

Snowshoe Thompson was glad, naturally. In his seventeen years on the routes, he'd got only $80.26 from the U.S. government. If it hadn't been for a few generous miners and their families, he'd have gone hungry. Occasionally the postmasters collected a dollar or two from people who posted letters, and

Thompson managed to squeeze a few pennies from those who received mail. The postmasters certainly liked him, and they sometimes wrote about Thompson to Washington, D.C. The replies were always courteous, but nothing came.

In the last few years, Thompson had no longer pressed his claims. He was just too good-humored, and even his wife said that people took advantage of him. One postmaster who had the mail contract kept the money that was due to Thompson. Another postmaster, whom Thompson had assisted one spring, went bankrupt and never paid his debts.

Thompson's marriage may have changed his attitude. Money wasn't very important in the country where he'd grown up, but here in America it was different. Especially for a family man. And now the moment had come when he would finally be able to do something nice for Agnes and Arthur.

The leaders in Carson City suggested just one step. Could Thompson take the petition to Washington, D.C.? The signatures would make an impression, but if he went in person, it would be even better. A hearing would be held by the U.S. Senate. The senior Nevada Senator—the same James Nye who'd once been Nevada territory governor—would make a plea to the Committee on Post Offices, and Thompson should be present.

The sooner the better.

So on January 16, 1872, Thompson kissed his wife good-bye, strapped a suitcase to his back, and traveled to Reno, Nevada. The next day he boarded the Union Pacific train. It had several fancy Pullman sleeping cars, built with fine woods and hung with curtains between the bunks. But that was too expensive; thrifty John Thompson chose to sit on one of the straight-backed benches instead. Soon the train whistled and clattered toward the east in a wake of steam from the locomotive's high smoke-stacks. Soon, too, the coaches were in the middle of a blizzard that drove snow mixed with coal dust against Thompson's window. The journey proved slower than anticipated. It took three days to get to the hilly, barren country 35 miles west of Laramie City, in Wyoming territory. Thompson's train stopped; it had got stuck in the drifts. The brakemen and engineers stumbled from car to car asking for volunteers to shovel snow. Many men kept silent. Not Thompson. He was among the first to go out into his element. He shoveled a full day along with a few others. The train edged forward another few miles, then stopped again. Once more the crews came to get Thompson. Would he help some more? If they could only reach a nearby depot, the train would be all right. All they needed were more locomotives. But when they puffed into the depot 20 miles west of Laramie City, the extra engines didn't help either. The snow was just too high. The train would no longer budge. The railroad people tried plows, but to no avail.

Thompson returned to his carriage, which shook in the storm. He ate some food Agnes had packed for him. He talked to railroad personnel. He listened to other passengers. He watched the swirling, hissing snow.

But he must have felt impatient. If he didn't take his petition to Washington soon, the politicians might change their minds about him. The people in the nation's capital had tight schedules.

Snowshoe Thompson waited out the night. By morning he made up his mind. He would walk to Laramie City, from where he might catch another train east. He told a few other passengers about his plan. They agreed that they might be stranded in the train for days, but it was madness to venture into the fierce weather. Only one man thought that the gamble was worth it. His name was Rufus Turner, and he, too, had an urgent appointment in the East.

Thompson and Turner left the train that Monday morning. At once the wind blasted against their bodies, almost toppling them. But Thompson strode ahead, bent in two, breaking trail. On skis it would have been difficult enough. But afoot each step through the deep whiteness was agony. The bitter cold clawed at the men's faces, and the baggage on their backs made travel even rougher. Their eyebrows and beards were soon crusted with snow, and their clothes looked like white sheets. After about 10 miles, Turner hollered for Thompson to stop. "Suitcase—too heavy." The Norwegian took the other man's luggage and fought on. The snow was still falling, and Thompson could see very little. But he kept to the visible line of the railroad tracks. This way, they would not get lost. There were no houses at all here, and in any case they would have been blotted out by snow. Mile after mile, the two men struggled across the railroad ties.

You might have thought that their ordeal would never end, but before darkness Thompson and Turner knew they had won. They reached Laramie City, which is now called Laramie. The situation was critical. In the railroad yards they passed still another marooned train. The 80,000-pound locomotive was dead, and the snow went up to the windowsills of the carriages. In the city no one dared out of the houses. All the stables were shut, and the streets were a mess of snow and abandoned wagons. There had been no school that day, and the churches,

too, were shrouded by snow. A thermometer read thirty below zero.

Turner suggested they should have a hot drink and food and a little warmth, so the two men entered the Union Pacific Railroad Hotel, across from the railroad station. They came in time to find the long tables of the dining hall filled with diners and busy waitresses, who carried thick mugs of coffee. The two men got some information along with their dinners. Bad news. There would be no transportation to Cheyenne, Wyoming. Not for several days, anyway. This was logical, for right then only one line—the Transcontinental Railroad—spanned the West. And this one line was "blockaded," or snowbound. In the Laramie station yet another Union Pacific train was stuck. Outside the hotel the wind didn't cease blowing.

Thompson later described the evil weather to his friend De Quille. But even the local Laramie newspaper bore him out. An account in the *Daily Sentinel* read: "Today, the wind rose to a tempest. Snow twisted in all directions and flew in a thousand shifting eddies to the right, left, front, rear, near the surface and upwards. Snow forced its way into every crack and cranny. The citizens lost their way half a block from their houses. . . ."

By morning the blizzard had let up only slightly, and Thompson's companion decided to wait it out in Laramie. He had been able to get one of the Railroad Hotel's 65 rooms, and he would stay until trains ran again. Turner would be in for a long wait. But not Thompson. After a night's sleep in Laramie, he was ready for the outdoors again. He just wouldn't give up.

Cheyenne was 56 miles away. Surely there would be trains east from Cheyenne. Thompson took his suitcase and performed an almost incredible feat. He bucked the icy winds and walked up and down the Medicine Bow Mountains, crossed and recrossed the timber, and followed the rail line down the rolling shelterless prairie all the way to Cheyenne. A distance of 56 miles. It was pure Thompson, pure Jon Torsteinson Rui, which had once been his name. And the performance was doubly remarkable for a man of forty-six, which was considered old in those days. No, age had not lost him his determination.

People were astonished when they saw him the first night out of Laramie at the Buford Station, but the citizens of Cheyenne were even more surprised. Mountaineer outruns the iron horse! read one newspaper's headline. He was the first man in two weeks who'd got through from Nevada. In an interview he declared that he'd have done better on his skis. Cheyenne was a boomtown during those years, thanks to the railroad. But that day no one would have guessed it! Cheyenne was out of coal, and many people sat in freezing houses. A local paper, the Cheyenne *Daily Leader,* ran big advertisements for "shawls and cloaks"; the weather was billed as "very cold, bleak and boisterous," an especially disagreeable day when Thompson arrived.

While Thompson's startling accomplishment made news all over the East, too, the mail carrier already sat on a Union Pacific train that took him out of Cheyenne. The train rattled through the vast country to Omaha, toward the Missouri River, and finally to Washington, D.C. He needn't have hurried so. The Senators were glad to see him, but they took their time with the petition he'd brought. Postal officials were cordial, just as their letters had been.

It took awhile for action, though. In Congress there were

several important matters ahead of Thompson's. He turned up in the gallery to listen in. Senators were busy arguing about Utah, which wanted statehood. The Civil War over, Senators had to debate the South's reconstruction. A Senator suggested a new Marine hospital for San Francisco. "The lawmaking here goes very slow," Thompson wrote his wife. Apparently Thompson's document would soon be studied and voted upon. Patience.

Meanwhile Thompson must have felt ill at ease in the capital. His old-fashioned, wide-lapeled suit was clean, but the people here were much better dressed. The rich rode about in graceful carriages pulled by two horses. Thompson was on foot. Nor could he match the gentlemen's top hats. The Washingtonians wore elegant shoes, whereas the man from Carson Valley had only his buffalo boots. He went to a shop and inquired about more fashionable footgear. The prices hit him with more force than the Wyoming winds. So he never bought shoes.

His lodging was more expensive than it would have been in the West. After a few weeks he found a cheaper room and limited himself to two modest meals a day. Despite his painful waiting, he thought of his family. "Tell Arthur to be a good boy while I'm gone and I will bring him something," he said in a letter to Agnes.

After many weeks Thompson was finally invited to the Senate hearing. He read the eloquent report about himself. "Twice a month with regularity John Thompson performed the perilous journey over the Sierra Nevada Mountains, traveling on snowshoes, with a mail averaging forty pounds on his back. For a distance of sixty miles there was no habitation on the way, and all traces of the road were obliterated by snows from fifteen to twenty feet deep; and all travel obstructed for five or six months in the year. No person save Thompson could be found who was willing, under these circumstances, to transport the mails across the mountains; and he was induced to do it only by the urgent solicitations of the people of Carson Valley, and the hope that in the future he might be paid for his services."

But in the Forty-second Congress of the United States the promised $6,000 had already shrunk. For unknown reasons the U.S. Post Office officials suggested that Thompson should be paid for only one season's mail carrying. The figure was to be $750, from which someone deducted the $80.22 which he'd already been paid, leaving the sum of $669.78.

Thompson waited for several more weeks in Washington for this small amount while his own savings were dwindling. His back pay never came. The mail carrier made the rounds to find out just what happened. No one is sure today, except that the politicians talked much and did little. "I can wait no longer," he wrote to Agnes, adding in his warmhearted way: "The men are all very kind here and I know they are doing everything they can for me. But it takes more time than I can spare. I'm needed at home."

Idle sitting just wasn't for him, and that March he took a train back to Nevada. Was he very sad? No one knows for sure. Perhaps he consoled himself with the many signatures on the petition; it was proof that people believed in him. Being a mature person, Thompson must have also known that life cannot fulfill every wish and that even the best plans sometimes just don't pan out. Dan De Quille, the man who perhaps knew him best, judged that Thompson's work carried its own reward. The mail deliveries were more important than dollars and filled him with pride. "It was like going forth to battle," the wise

De Quille wrote. "And each successive trip was a victory."

Deep within him, Thompson had reasons to be satisfied. Everyone knew him as a dependable man. To carry the mails in the first place he'd once signed a paper that asked him to work with "celerity, certainty, security." And he had done so, year after year. He was brave and honest and decent, which all seemed more important than the sparse money. And of course Thompson still had his family—the beaming, lively son and the ever-patient wife.

To support them, Thompson continued homesteading. He cared for the livestock, which, as far as is known, consisted of one horse, two oxen, and some pigs. He took jobs in sawmills and toward the end of his life briefly became a mining superintendent. Thompson was never paid for his post office labors, but the people still cried out for him. Especially young people. They wanted him to build skis, and he complied. They wanted him to organize races, which he did. They wanted him to put up small purses for the winners, which he did, too.

Even as he aged, Thompson was the one summoned in a crisis. One of his last exploits started one night when a California widow sent a friend to the mail carrier. A bad thing had happened, the man said. The widow's son, a boy named Roddy Carpenter, had broken his arm. Skiing. The doctor was with him, but Roddy wouldn't let him touch the arm unless Snowshoe Thompson came. Could he? Tonight? It was about 16 miles of tortuous skiing to Silver Mountain and the widow's house. Of course, as always, it stormed. And of course, the aging, graying John Thompson made it.

He had to.

He was Snowshoe Thompson to the end.

XI Gone but Not Forgotten

SPRING HAD COME to Carson Valley. The Carson River moved swiftly again, made bold by the melting snows. Sierra waterfalls, after an all-winter freeze, came crashing through the last icicles. Lake Tahoe shone bluer than ever, and under the last snows of Carson Pass, which Thompson had sometimes crossed in moonlight, mountain flowers now waited to push through. White still glinted from 10,067-foot Monument Peak; Thompson had got to know it intimately on his many trips to Placerville. Everywhere, the pines turned a lighter, brighter green, scrubbed by old man winter. Spring was coming! On Genoa Peak tiny shoots of mountain grasses slept under the snow cover. The first buds soon graced the chestnut trees in Genoa.

People had come and gone, but with all the mining activity Genoa was flourishing. James Sisson, whose life Thompson had saved, had grown tired of the region and moved to one of the Atlantic states. He was to outlive Thompson. Several of the rescuers who had been along, shoving that leaden sled twenty years ago, were dead now. The Mormon-built stockade was still there, but that spring the snow had vanished around the thick wood posts and the fencing. Genoa's streets bustled with men.

John Thompson had seen the town grow. Gold Hill was a busy place of 10,000 inhabitants. Virginia City was miles of thin shanties and barracks, but also rows upon rows of stone houses and brick buildings. There were jewel strings of ornate mansions, all curtained and wallpapered, with velvety couches and rosewood beds and adorned mirrors and ebony-black pianos. One Virginia City club possessed ten thousand dollars' worth of furniture and paintings. Some ladies wore exquisitely embroidered dresses and carried delicate umbrellas, and wealthy gentlemen arrived on stages in elegant suits and vests. Furriers and jewelry stores did well, and the rich clamored for arts. Famous opera singers and celebrated actors therefore sought out Virginia City, which had a population of some 25,000. Theater life was brisk. Restaurants employed chefs from Europe, who did wonders with venison meat.

The rich amused themselves at fancy balls, but without Thompson. Nor was he known to go to the billiard tables that had sprung up all over town, or to gamble, or to join the miners' nightly pastime of drinking in one of the 110 saloons. To the end, no one saw Thompson in a honky-tonk.

In some Virginia City buildings real elevators creaked up and down. The *Territorial Enterprise,* which once employed Thompson's services as carrier of printing equipment, now rumbled with all sorts of newfangled presses. Dan De Quille still worked for the newspaper, which prospered. Indeed, the Comstock Lode and silver mining had turned Virginia City into one of America's richest cities. The wagons rolled and rolled out of the Comstock; in all, there would be three hundred million dollars' worth of ore, and despite some ups and downs, the wealth was beyond compare. Thompson had never cashed in. But he was not one to envy the others; jealousy was a foreign word to him.

Indeed, he witnessed some astonishing success stories. Among them was that of Mrs. Bowers, Thompson's friend. He had never found a crystal ball for her, but she managed to predict her own good future all the same. It all started when Mrs. Bowers married a prospector, who wanted to sell his claim. Mrs. Bowers counseled him to hold onto it, and the couple—to Thompson's astonishment—made $1,000,000 from silver in a single year. They built a mansion, which still stands there, and they lived extravagantly. After the death of her husband Mrs. Bowers promptly took a trip to England, from where she brought back twenty thousand dollars' worth of jewels. Then she herself died.

By 1876 Virginia City had four banks and fifty dry-goods stores, and Thompson saw the wealth even spill into the streets, where horses galloped on silver shoes. Men made fortunes by freighting, and grocers became incredibly prosperous by selling food to everyone at inflated prices. There were plenty of customers for every trade because people came from all over the world to visit Virginia City. A special train now connected this metropolis and Carson City, with six tunnels in between.

Trains now not only ran to the East, but the Sierra Nevadas were also bridged by railroads to the West. In Virginia City and elsewhere Thompson saw posters announcing the train to San Francisco. LIGHTNING EXPRESS! read the headline. In bright lettering, the poster promised LUXURIOUS CARS! and reminded any doubters to AVOID THE DANGERS OF THE SEA! And what a train it was! When it roared in from Omaha, stopping with great noise in Virginia City, travelers often got on just to try the luxurious sleeping accommodations.

A train crossed Donner Pass, where starving men had eaten the flesh of the dead members of their party a few decades ago; trains kept steaming to Folsom and Sacramento and San Francisco. This Central Pacific Railroad, finished in 1869, was all the more remarkable for its construction crews, some of whom Thompson must have seen in Carson Valley. They were Chinese, about 15,000 of them, slight of build but able to work twelve to fourteen hours a day at a little more than $7 a week.

Thompson himself had been on the train east from Reno and had seen the freights that carried loads of merchandise. During the last few years better snowplows made this transportation run almost as punctually as he had on skis. In Carson City almost anything from coconuts to the finest crockery could now be bought. Mail was reliably delivered by railroad via special mail cars. Instead of requiring three months by ship, a letter from San Francisco reached New York in about twelve days. The telegraph had also long come to stay, clicking away from coast to coast. That April, 1876, Snowshoe Thompson put away his skis for good. He had a notion that his services would no longer be needed. Besides, there was work to do on his little farm, 30 miles south of Carson City, in the Diamond Valley. It had never yielded any riches either. But Thompson's fields stood neatly plowed, and money or not, Thompson believed in doing a job well. In early May it was again time for buying seed. Thompson and his nine-year-old Arthur trotted to town to bring back the bags. Early the next morning Thompson was ready for planting. His good wife Agnes saw him carry the sacks. "John," she asked, "are you sick?"

John Thompson did not answer. But after ten years of marriage wives have a way of knowing. Thompson shivered. Then he was hot. His blue eyes had fever written in them. His body shook with a sudden weakness. Thompson, the Norwegian, was not one to complain. And, as usual, he wasn't one to give in. The wheat had to be planted. The day, May 14, was cloudy and windy, but he went out all the same.

Thompson saddled his horse and did his sowing from the saddle. That afternoon after he was done, perspiration ran through his blond beard. He was also coughing badly. Agnes talked him into going to bed. Doctors were not very efficient in those days, although they did come to a patient's home, which they seldom do now. No one knows for sure whether Thompson's illness was pneumonia or some sort of liver ailment. In any case, his devoted wife fed him medications. She massaged his chest and tenderly dried his wet forehead, and at night she stayed awake by his bedside. Still, his body was racked by pain.

John Thompson died in the afternoon of May 15, a Tuesday. From his bed, up to the last minute, he could see the Sierras he loved so much. Mountains had been his be-all and end-all, and the simple need of seeing mountains lasted until he shut his eyes.

His life's pleasures had been simple too: the quiet of the peaks, motion for his body, snow for a thirsty tongue, a slice of dried meat to still the hunger, a fire for his cold hands. He could warm his mind by reading a few pages in the Bible, which he had often done. He had hoped to do well for his wife's and son's sake, but it did not bother Thompson much that he had never made great sums of money. Other famous Westerners, great explorers like Daniel Boone or California gold discoverers like John Augustus Sutter, died poor, too. Their reward was worth more than gold. This was well said by David Henry Thoreau, the American writer and philosopher, who was born ten years earlier than Thompson. Before he died, Thoreau wrote: "An efficient man does what he can, whether the community pays him for it or not." Perhaps he had never heard of Thompson, but the words have great meaning all the same.

Snowshoe Thompson himself, like these men, must have realized that he had performed well on earth. He gave himself fully to others, and in his calm mountain way he was much more of a hero than the noisy, gun-toting outlaws. Thompson despised violence. He disliked the selfish because he was selfless himself. For this, and for his strength, he was respected by others. Jack Schaefer, a very good modern writer, called him simply a "good man of the West" and a "hero without glory." So Thompson's mother had been right, after all, when she told him, "Perhaps there's something more out there. Something that only you can do."

After Thompson's passing, word traveled all over the globe about him. Many people marveled at his courage. But to the Scandinavians, though they admired him, Thompson's outdoor stamina seemed only natural. For instance, Fridtjof Nansen, another Norwegian, was fifteen years old just then. He was to become a famous Polar explorer. Roald Amundsen, who discovered the South Pole, was four when his countryman of the High Sierras died.

Of course, there were also many stories about Snowshoe Thompson in American newspapers. But in the end, Dan De Quille, the Virginia City reporter and Thompson's friend, summed it up best of all. "Thompson's equal will probably never again be seen," De Quille wrote in 1876. "It would be hard to find another man combining his courage, physique, and powers of endurance—a man with such thews and sinews, controlled by such a will. There was no recklessness in anything he did."

This was as true in De Quille's days as it is now. Where Thompson pushed upward on foot, there are aerial tramways now because the modern skier does not like to climb mountains. He wants only to go downhill as fast as possible. Thompson's mail-carrying region is now covered with lifts of other kinds, too, consisting of chairs by the hundreds and gondolas that look like plastic eggs.

Thompson was certainly admired in the Sierras. In time, ski races would be named after him. His skis would go on display at Sutter's Fort in Sacramento, California, and then at the Plumas Eureka State Park, in the same state. Other relics went to the Holmenkollen Ski Museum in Oslo, Norway. For a while Thompson's log cabin in Diamond Valley became a shrine for visitors. Even the U.S. Post Office in faraway Washington, D.C., which had treated Thompson wretchedly, issued a stamp in his memory. Children stopped with their parents in Genoa, where they could see some of Thompson's sparse belongings and pictures of him—in a tiny museum. Men traveled all the way from Scandinavia to Thompson's resting place. A few years ago, a Norwegian ski team laid down a plaque in his honor, and people still bring flowers.

Snowshoe Thompson was buried in Genoa, Nevada, which has since become a quiet little hamlet. Thompson's wife and son rest next to him. They are still there. So is the cemetery, slanting up from a country road, blending with the steep slope, and then flowing into a forest of pines. Thompson's grave is flanked by an apple tree. Over the spot where he sleeps forever, a white stone monument holds a vigil. Skillfully chiseled into the granite is a pair of crossed skis.

If you come that way, you can read the inscription. NATIVE OF NORWAY, it reads. DEPARTED THIS LIFE MAY 15, 1876. GONE BUT NOT FORGOTTEN.

The marker on his grave misspelled Thompson's name, but the indistinct line at the bottom is more accurate. It reads "Gone but not forgotten."

Index

The Author

CURTIS CASEWIT has skied many trails in the world. Born in Germany, he has been to the Apennine Mountains in Italy, the Atlas Mountains in Africa, the Austrian Alps, the California Sierras, and the Rocky Mountains. Author of more than a dozen books, and contributor to many magazines, Mr. Casewit lives in Denver, Colorado, with his wife and three children.